LORE OF THE LAKES

Told in Story and Picture

TWILIGHT CALM

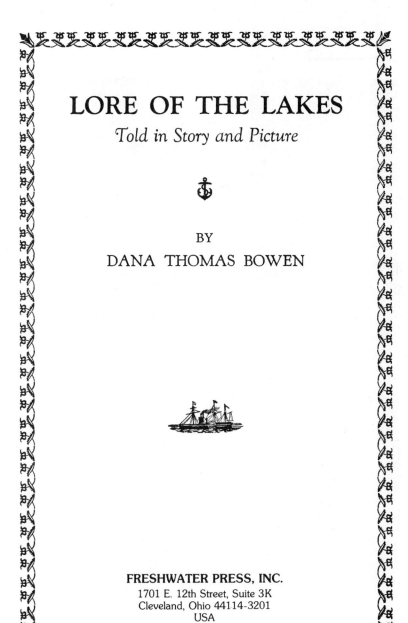

LORE OF THE LAKES

Told in Story and Picture

BY

DANA THOMAS BOWEN

FRESHWATER PRESS, INC.

1701 E. 12th Street, Suite 3K
Cleveland, Ohio 44114-3201
USA

BY DANA THOMAS BOWEN
PRINTED IN THE UNITED STATES OF AMERICA
FIRST PUBLISHED, SEPTEMBER, 1940
SECOND PRINTING, NOVEMBER, 1941
THIRD PRINTING, NOVEMBER, 1944
FOURTH PRINTING, OCTOBER, 1945
FIFTH PRINTING, DECEMBER, 1948
SIXTH PRINTING, JANUARY, 1958
SEVENTH PRINTING, NOVEMBER, 1962
EIGHTH PRINTING, DECEMBER, 1966
NINTH PRINTING, SEPTEMBER, 1969
TENTH PRINTING, JANUARY, 1973
ELEVENTH PRINTING, SEPTEMBER, 1976
TWELFTH PRINTING, MARCH, 1989

LIBRARY OF CONGRESS CATALOGUE CARD NUMBER: 40-33309

CONTENTS

DEDICATION XV

PREFACE 1

A WORD OF EXPLANATION 3

ONE—PARADE OF THE YEARS 5

TWO—DID YOU KNOW THAT . . .? 23

THREE—THE *Griffin* 31

FOUR—THE UNITED STATES BRIG *Niagara* . . 35

FIVE—THE *Walk-in-the-Water* 42

SIX—*Wolverine* 49

SEVEN—EARLY PASSENGER SHIPS AND LATER ONES 58

EIGHT—PICTORIAL SECTION 81

NINE—LAKE STEAMER STACKS AND U. S.
WEATHER BUREAU SIGNALS 148

TEN—THE CARAVELS OF CHRISTOPHER
COLUMBUS 161

ELEVEN—SAILED AWAY 165

TWELVE—THE *Tashmoo* AND *City of Erie* RACE . 180

CONTENTS (Cont.)

THIRTEEN—THE BIG STORM 189

FOURTEEN—THE STEAMER *Eastland* . . . 201

FIFTEEN—BLACK FRIDAY 209

SIXTEEN—THE FREIGHTER 218

SEVENTEEN—TODAY'S PASSENGER FLEET . . 241

EIGHTEEN—THE PASSENGER STEAMER *Seeandbee* . 256

NINETEEN—THE BURNING OF THE STEAMER
City of Buffalo 266

TWENTY—SAILOR YARNS 272

TWENTY-ONE—
LIST OF MAJOR DISASTERS ON THE LAKES . . 302

TABLE OF SAILING DISTANCES ON THE
GREAT LAKES 306

TABLE OF SAILING TIME BETWEEN PRINCIPAL
LAKE PORTS 307

SCALE OF STATUTE AND NAUTICAL MILES . . 308

ROMAN NOTATION 309

INDEX 311

ILLUSTRATIONS

TWILIGHT CALM . . . . Frontispiece

HAPPY ECHOES 81

Griffin 82

BATTLE OF LAKE ERIE SCENE 83

Niagara IN CLEVELAND 84

REBUILDING Niagara 85

SCHOONER Henry C. Richards 85

GREAT LAKES SCHOONER 86

OLD STATE LOCK AT THE SOO 86

THE Our Son 87

SCHOONER C. K. Clint 88

DETROIT HARBOR IN 1836 89

SCHOONER Hattie Hutt 90

Walk-in-the-Water 91

EARLY SOO LOCK 92

EARLY STEAMER IN SOO LOCK 93

U. S. S. Michigan 94

U. S. S. Wolverine 95

Vandalia—FIRST PROPELLER 96

TUG Samson AND THE FIVE TOWS 96

EARLY FREIGHTER Harlem 97

Island Queen—CIVIL WAR DAYS PASSENGER STEAMER . . 98

Onoko—EARLY IRON FREIGHTER 98

ILLUSTRATIONS (Cont.)

C. F. Curtis—WOODEN LUMBER STEAMER 99

PASSENGER STEAMER Japan 100

India—AS A BARGE TODAY 101

Orinoco—WOODEN FREIGHTER 101

Marshall F. Butters—WOODEN LUMBER STEAMER . . . 102

City of Glasgow—WOODEN BULK FREIGHTER . . . 103

BARGE Abyssinia 103

PASSENGER WHALEBACK Christopher Columbus . . . 104

Yakima—FIRST FREIGHTER TO CARRY ELECTRIC
LIGHTS ON LAKES 105

Superior City—STEEL BULK FREIGHTER 105

PASSENGER SHIP North West AT THE SOO 106

THE North West 107

Eastland IN HER HEYDAY 108

U. S. S. Wilmette AT PRESENT 109

Eastland ON LAKE ERIE 110

OPENING OF DAVIS LOCK IN 1914 110

Bannockburn—LAKE SUPERIOR'S "FLYING DUTCHMAN" . 111

WHALEBACK James B. Colgate, LOST ON LAKE ERIE . . 112

EARLY WOODEN SHIPBUILDING YARD 113

SANDUSKY PASSENGER DOCKS ABOUT 1885 TO 1890 . . 114

A. Wehrle, Jr.—LAKE ERIE PLEASURE BOAT OF THE 90'S . 115

Arrow—LAKE ERIE ISLANDS PASSENGER STEAMER . . . 115

FACSIMILE OF JUDGES' LETTER ON Tashmoo AND
City of Erie RACE 116

X

ILLUSTRATIONS (Cont.)

DETROIT WATER FRONT ABOUT 1910 117

PASSENGER STEAMER *City of Erie* 117

PASSENGER STEAMER *Frank E. Kirby* 118

END OF THE *I. Watson Stephenson*, LUMBER STEAMER . 118

Tionesta—PASSENGER SHIP RECENTLY DE-COMMISSIONED . 119

North Lake—FREIGHTER CAUGHT IN WINTER BLOW . . 120

FREIGHTERS CAUGHT IN ICE AT THE SOO 120

THANKSGIVING DAY ON A FREIGHTER 121

APRIL NAVIGATION ON THE LAKES 121

James Carruthers—CANADIAN FREIGHTER LOST . . . 122

Hydrus—LOST IN "BIG STORM" 123

Leafield—LOST IN "BIG STORM" 123

John A. McGean—LOST IN "BIG STORM" 124

Regina—LOST IN "BIG STORM" 124

COMPOSITE PHOTO OF STEAMER *Chas. S. Price*—

    LOST IN "BIG STORM" 125

Isaac M. Scott—LOST IN "BIG STORM" 126

L. C. Waldo—LOST IN "BIG STORM" 126

Wexford—LOST IN "BIG STORM" 127

Argus—LOST IN "BIG STORM" 127

Kamloops—FREIGHTER DISAPPEARED IN LAKE SUPERIOR . 128

Wm. H. Wolf—STEAMER UPBOUND IN SOO LOCKS . . 129

WRECKING WHALEBACK FREIGHTER *J. T. Reid* . . . 129

Wm. A. Paine—FREIGHTER LEAVING SOO LOCK . . . 130

FREIGHTERS LOCKING UP AT SOO LOCKS 130

XI

ILLUSTRATIONS (Cont.)

STEAMER City of Buffalo AFTER THE FIRE 131

STEAMER City of Buffalo LATER STRIPPED TO MAIN DECK . 131

PERRY MONUMENT AT PUT-IN-BAY 132

STEAMER Jas. A. Farrell AND Seeandbee AT THE SOO . . 133

STEAMER Chas. L. Hutchinson—TYPICAL MODERN
BULK FREIGHTER 133

AIR VIEW OF THE SOO LOCKS 134

EXCURSION STEAMER Put-In-Bay 135

PASSENGER STEAMER Seeandbee AT A SOO DOCK . . . 136

STEAMER Seeandbee AT MACKINAC ISLAND 137

BOW VIEW OF STEAMER City of Detroit III 137

PLEASURE CRUISE SHIP South American 138

PASSENGER STEAMER Noronic 139

PASSENGER STEAMER Alabama 139

PASSENGER STEAMER Greater Buffalo 140

PASSENGER STEAMER City of Cleveland III 141

CARFERRY Windsor AT DETROIT 142

CANAL MOTOR-SHIP Clevelander 142

STEAMER Carl D. Bradley—LARGEST FREIGHTER . . . 143

STEAMER Governor Miller 144

STEAMER Lemoyne—CANADIAN BULK FREIGHTER . . . 145

STEAMER Harry Coulby 146

STREAMLINED CARFERRY—City of Midland—(DRAWING) . 147

VESSEL STACKS . . 148-149-150-151-152-153-154-155-156-157

U. S. WEATHER BUREAU STORM WARNINGS 158

PROFILE OF THE GREAT LAKES 160

DEDICATION

To my never failing friend and father-in-law, Charles Joseph Snow, of Cleveland, who always enjoyed and never tired of talking ships with me, and whose knowledge and inspiration has so helped me in preparing this work, I affectionately dedicate this book. My only regret is that I have written it too late to receive his comment.

Dana T Bowen

⚓ ⚓ ⚓ ⚓ ⚓ ⚓ ⚓ ⚓

PREFACE

Many, many volumes have been written of the ships that have sailed the seven salty seas, and their interest and enchantment is irresistible. From the primitive craft of the early Norsemen to the modern super-liner of today, man has always stood by, looked, wondered and thrilled. A ship is a wonderful thing. Man builds it and man sails it, and so conquers the vast watery wastes with it. Thrilling experiences are ever at hand. Lives hang in the balance. Fortunes are made and lost. Normal life everywhere depends on ships. To some a ship is life itself, to others it is a source of pleasure, education or travel. To countless others it offers entertainment, diversion, excitement and relaxation when its story is told between the covers of a book.

America's five Great Lakes and their tributaries, fresh water all, offer as thrilling tales of the ships that ply their waters as were ever written of the seas. Hard, sturdy men have sailed forth upon these lakes in many types of ships. Indians and early explorers used frail canoes, much the same as their distant native brothers did along the sea coasts. Ships on the lakes have developed and improved until today the modern Great Lakes freighter has no equal for tonnage and efficiency anywhere in the world.

Every ship has a story. Men wrap their lives about it, and women their loves, and in so doing it makes fiction

1

appear dull in comparison. Listen to a few of their stories as gathered from old sailors and young sailors, captains and engineers, owners and businessmen, all of them so vitally interested in their ships that sail America's Inland Seas.

* * *

It is the way of man to change things. He is ever seeking to improve and better his lot. So it is that his ships have changed. The ship that was launched yesterday and proudly acclaimed as the super ship is only a stepping stone to the one that is launched today. Into tomorrow's ships will be built all the experiences of the ships that have gone before.

Man changes his methods, his cargoes, his channels, and then he must change his ships to conform to them. All this presents a most entrancing procession of water craft as the years go by.

The old is quickly forgotten in the interest of the new; but, upon the wrecks, the struggles, the trials and the successes of the old, are built the new.

Let us therefore look upon a few of the ships of the Great Lakes, both the old and the new, before they pass into the forgotten realms of man's transportation efforts and try to catch a gleam of the enchantment as the parade of the ships goes past.

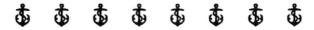

A WORD OF EXPLANATION

Obviously a great amount of the material in a work such as this must be gathered from many sources. Men familiar with the lakes were interviewed, others contacted by correspondence. Endless records and voluminous details were reviewed, carefully selected and checked for accuracy, and every effort made to have the accounts correct. Where the records did not tally, honest effort was made to present herein what appeared to be the most correct and logical. However, errors may have crept into the work despite every effort to the contrary. If such is found the author asks your pardon and kind indulgence.

CHAPTER ONE

THE PARADE OF THE YEARS

1492—Christopher Columbus discovered America.

1513—Balboa discovered the Pacific Ocean.

1535—Jacques Cartier sailed up the St. Lawrence River for the French.

1608—Samuel de Champlain founded Quebec.

1615—Champlain discovered Lake Huron, at the French River in Georgian Bay. THIS WAS THE RECOGNIZED DISCOVERY OF THE GREAT LAKES.

1620—*Mayflower* landed on Plymouth Rock, Cape Cod.

1629—Brule discovered Lake Superior.

1632—Champlain made a rough chart of the lakes.

1634—Jean Nicolet explored Les Cheneaux Islands and discovered Lake Michigan.

1641—Fathers Jogues and Raymbault established a mission at the Soo.

1655—French fur traders Radisson and Groseilliers entered the Lake Superior Country.

1668—Father Marquette founded a mission at the Soo.

1669—Lake Erie discovered by Joliet.

1670—Radisson formed the Hudson Bay Trading Company.

1673—La Salle crudely mapped the Great Lakes.

5

1678—La Salle commenced the first recorded voyage by ship on the waters of the Great Lakes, on Lake Ontario.

1679—Daniel Greysolon, Sieur Du Lhut, landed at site of Duluth, which later was named for him.
La Salle started out for the upper lakes in the *Griffin*. (Aug. 7th).
Griffin set out on return voyage and was never heard of. (Sept. 18).

1701—Cadillac visited site of Detroit.

1754—Start of the French and Indian War.

1755—The British built several ships of war on Lake Ontario.

1756—French forces captured British control over the lakes.

1760—British regained control over the lakes.
Detroit surrendered to England.

1763—End of the French and Indian War.
Canada ceded to England.   British warships, schooners *Huron* and *Michigan,* in service on Lake Erie.

1775—Revolutionary War commenced.

1776—Declaration of Independence adopted.

1779—British built a fort at Mackinac Island.

1781—End of fighting in Revolutionary War. Cornwallis surrendered.

1783—Peace of Paris signed, ending the Revolutionary War.

1785—Sloop *Otter* first vessel to navigate Lake Superior.

THE PARADE OF THE YEARS

1787—John Fitch operated first steam vessel in United States on the Delaware River, using paddles.

1788—United States Constitution adopted.

1789—Schooner *Nancy* built at Detroit.
George Washington inaugurated as first president of the United States.

1790—Legislation approved creating the Revenue Marine —the present U. S. Coast Guard.

1794—Act to found the United States Navy.

1796—First U. S. armed vessel appeared on the lakes, the *Detroit*.
Moses Cleaveland settled in Cleveland.

1798—Northwest Fur Co. built first crude lock at the Soo.

1807—Robert Fulton sailed the *Clermont* on the Hudson River. Acclaimed as first steamboat.
U. S. Coast Survey organized.

1809—John Jacob Astor, a German, founded American Fur Company.
Steamer *Accommodation*, first on record to sail freshwater of the lakes, ran from Montreal to Quebec.

1811—First steamboat built to operate on the Mississippi River.

1812—Start of the War of 1812 against England.

1813—Commodore Oliver Hazard Perry's victory in the Battle of Lake Erie on Sept. 10th. U. S. obtained right to the lakes.

1814—Treaty of Ghent signed ending War of 1812.

1815—Commercial activities commenced on the Great Lakes.

1816—Work started on the Erie Canal.

Steamer *Frontenac* launched in Lake Ontario.

U. S. Coast Survey began operations.

1817—Steamer *Ontario* launched in Lake Ontario at Sacketts Harbor.

Rush-Bagot Agreement signed between Britain and United States.

John Jacob Astor established trading post at Duluth.

1818—*Walk-in-the-Water* launched at Black Rock, N. Y. Acclaimed as the first steamer to navigate the Great Lakes.

First U. S. lighthouse on Lakes built at Buffalo, N. Y.

1819—*Savannah,* first steamer to cross Atlantic, from Savannah, Ga., to Liverpool, England, in 30 days Sail and steam both used.

Commodore Oliver Hazard Perry died.

1820—Gov. Cass raised U. S. flag at the Soo, removing the British flag.

Influx of immigration into the lakes country.

1821—Steamer *Walk-in-the-Water* wrecked near Buffalo on Nov. 1st.

Marblehead light near Sandusky, O., established.

1822—Fort Brady (U. S.) built at the Soo.

Steamer *Superior* built to replace the *Walk-in-the-Water,* at Buffalo.

1825—Steamer *Henry Clay* launched. Third accredited lake steamer.

Work commenced on the Welland Canal between Lakes Erie and Ontario.

Fort Gratiot light at Port Huron, Mich., established.

1826—Erie Canal between Buffalo and Albany opened for service.

First steamer appeared on Lake Michigan, near Green Bay.

1827—Steamer *Frontenac* burned in Niagara River.

First railroad in United States chartered.

1829—Welland Canal opened for navigation.

First railroad locomotive used at Carbondale, Pa.

1830—Ohio Canal, Cleveland to Portsmouth, Ohio, on the Ohio River, was opened to navigation, 309 miles in length. Canal packets required 80 hours to make the trip, passing through the towns of Akron, Massillon, New Philadelphia, Coshocton, Newark, Chillicothe and Waverly.

1831—Steamer *United States*, largest American passenger boat on the lakes, launched at Ogdensburg, N. Y., 142 feet long and 26 feet beam.

First practical locomotive used.

1832—Chicago River light established. First light on Lake Michigan.

Steamer *Ontario*, early steamer, dismantled at Oswego, N. Y.

First street railway in United States commenced operation.

1833—Steamer *Michigan*, first with a cabin on the deck on the lakes, launched at Detroit.

Chicago received first charter as a city and port of entry.

1834—American Fur Co. built schooner *J. J. Astor* at the

Soo, first ship to fly U. S. flag on Lake Superior. First ship, schooner *Illinois,* arrived at Chicago from lower lakes.
Steamer *Washington* burned on maiden voyage off Dunkirk, N. Y.

1835—Era of new settling of lake country, particularly on Lake Erie.
Starting of commercial activity.
Steamer *Superior,* second on lakes, had engine removed and was converted into a sailing vessel.

1837—First floating lightship on lakes, in Straits of Mackinac.
Michigan became a State.
First locomotive to enter western Illinois delivered at Chicago by a sailing vessel.

1838—Ships' screw propeller patented.
U. S. Steamboat Inspection Service established by Congress.
Steamers *Sirius* and *Great Western* crossed the Atlantic.

1839—Regular line of eight boats operated from Buffalo to Chicago.
Brig *Osceola* loaded first bulk cargo of grain from Chicago.

1840—Steamer *Vandalia* built at Oswego, N. Y. First commercial propeller on the lakes and in the world. Also first steamboat to have the engines aft.

1841—Steamer *Erie* burned in Lake Erie. 175 lost. First sideway launching took place.

10

THE PARADE OF THE YEARS

United States Lake Survey started.

1842—Commenced a period of intense rivalry for patronage among lake boats.
Steamer *Oswego*, second propeller ship built on Lake Ontario.

1843—The steam whistle first used on the Great Lakes.
U.S.S. Michigan (now *Wolverine*) launched at Erie, Pa.
Schooner *Dolphin* ran from Great Lakes to New Orleans, via Ohio Canal, Ohio and Mississippi Rivers.
Ship *Superior* lost in a gale.

1844—Iron discovered near Negaunee, Mich.
Copper discovered in the Lake Superior Country.
Passenger steamer *Empire* built at Cleveland; largest and finest yet built on the lakes. Brigantine *Pacific* voyaged from Toronto to Liverpool with flour.
U.S.S. Michigan made her first cruise.
Morse telegraph first used.

1845—First iron merchant vessel built in Canada, the *Richelieu*.
United States Naval Academy opened.

1846—Steamer *Julia Palmer* hauled overland at the Soo into Lake Superior.

1847—St. Lawrence River canal system completed, permitting ships to sail from lakes to the sea.
Rivers and Harbors Congress held in Chicago—the start of modern harbors on the lakes.

11

Steamer *Phoenix* burned in Lake Michigan near Sheboygan—240 lost.

1848—Wisconsin became a State.

1849—Barquentine *Eureka* left Cleveland for San Francisco and the California gold fields, via St. Lawrence River, Atlantic and Pacific Ocean around Cape Horn, and arrived safely.

1850—Transportation boom started on the Great Lakes. Steamer *G. P. Griffin* burned in Lake Erie near Cleveland—94 lost.

1851—"King Strang" created a "kingdom" on Beaver Island in Lake Michigan, which was quelled by the *U. S. S. Michigan.*

1852—Railroad completed between Cleveland and Toledo. First U. S. Lake Survey charts published. Steamer *Atlantic* sank after a collision with steamer *Ogdensburgh* near Long Point in Lake Erie—250 lost.

1853—Passenger steamers *Crescent City, Queen of the West, Mississippi* and *Saint Lawrence* built. Famous race between steamers *Mississippi* and *Queen of the West,* from Buffalo to Cleveland, latter ship won. Another race was run by the steamers *Queen City* and *Alabama* over the same course and was won by the *Queen City* which averaged almost 14½ miles per hour.

1854—Elegant passenger steamers *Western World* and *Plymouth Rock* built at Buffalo. Former ship was 348 feet long, with a deck width of 72 feet. The

Plymouth Rock was slightly smaller. These were the largest and finest afloat on the lakes.

First railroad completed into Windsor, Ontario.

1855—First State Lock at the Soo completed.

1856—Grand Trunk Railroad opened, Quebec to Montreal.

Passenger steamer *Western Metropolis* built on Lake Erie.

Steamer *Northern Indiana* burned off Point Pelee in Lake Erie. Many lives lost.

1857—107 sidewheel steamers on the lakes; 135 propeller steamers; and 1,006 sailing vessels of all classes.

Financial panic in lake transportation began.

Iron Mountain Railway in Upper Michigan Peninsula completed.

Steamer *Montreal* burned in St. Lawrence River, two miles off Lake Ontario—250 lost.

First passenger steamer *City of Buffalo* built.

1858—Atlantic cable laid.

1859—Schooner *J. F. Warner* sailed from Cleveland to Glasgow, Scotland.

1860—Excursion steamer *Lady Elgin* sank in Lake Michigan, between Chicago and Milwaukee, in a gale after being rammed by the schooner *Augusta*—287 lives lost.

1861—Start of the Civil War in United States.

"Halcyon Days" on the great lakes. Prosperity reigned. High rates and plentiful cargoes.

1862—Steamer *Merchant,* pioneer iron freight ship, started.
Steamer *North Star* burned. She held the record for speed on the lakes of 16 miles per hour.

1863—Elegant steamers *Western World* and similar ships were sold and dismantled.

1864—Era of sailing schooners on the Great Lakes.

1865—End of Civil War. Lee surrendered at Appomatox.
Steamer *Pewabic* sunk off Thunder Bay , Lake Huron, in collision with steamer *Meteor.*

1866—Michigan lumber shipping era commenced in large volume.
Prosperous tug towing era, notably in the Detroit rivers.
First Atlantic cable message sent.

1867—Big Sable Lighthouse erected on Lake Michigan.
"Anchor Line" on the lakes incorporated.

1868—Peak of sailing ship era on the lakes, 1,875 being listed.
Old D & C Line started operations with two boats.
Steamer *Seabird* burned in Lake Michigan—100 lives lost.
Steamer *Morning Star* sank in Lake Erie, off Lorain, in collision with sailing barge *Courtland*—26 lives lost.

1870—United States Weather Bureau established.
Steamer *R. J. Hackett* built, early ship to have engines aft.

1871—The great Chicago fire occurred.

Sister steamers *India, China* and *Japan* built; three famous ships all along the lakes, operating between Buffalo and Duluth, carrying passengers and freight. All three ships had long and successful careers.

First coal cargo taken to Duluth.

1872—First practical ore development on Menominee Range.

Schooner *Pamlico* sailed from Chicago to Liverpool, England, with grain.

Schooner *Lyman M. Davis* built in Muskegon, Mich. This vessel sailed the lakes for 60 years, outlasting several generations of lake seamen. She was burned as a spectacle at Toronto in the fall of 1933.

1874—Little Sable Lighthouse on Lake Michigan built.

Steamer *Merchant,* pioneer iron boat, lost on Lake Erie.

Schooner *J. I. Case* built at Manitowoc, Wis., sailed the lakes for 50 years mostly in the grain trade; obsolete at last, she was sunk in deep water near Quebec, Canada. Typical of her times, on one trip alone, from Chicago to Buffalo with grain, she carried 60,000 bushels of wheat at 7c per bushel and netted the tidy sum of $4,200 for the trip down the lakes. She carried no power other than sail.

1875—Mackinac Island became a National Park, 20 years later being ceded to Michigan as a State Park.

1878—First Steamer *City of Detroit* launched for D & C

Line. Composite hull.

1879—First incandescent light made.

1881—Wetzel Lock (No. 1) opened at the Soo. Lockage tolls abolished.
Five masted ship *David Dows* built at Toledo, Ohio; largest sailing vessel to be built on the lakes.
Steamer *Algomah* started ferry service at the Straits of Mackinac.

1882—Steamer *Onoko* launched at Cleveland; first iron bulk freighter on lakes. In her early years she used sails to assist her steam plant. Saw 33 years profitable service.

1883—Steamer *City of Mackinac* built for D & C Line.

1884—United States Bureau of Navigation created.
Standard time adopted in United States.

1886—Steamer *City of Cleveland II* launched for the D & C Lines.

1887—Heroic rescue of crew of schooner *James F. Joy*, which foundered off Ashtabula, by Captain Wm. Packer and a volunteer crew.

1889—Alexander McDougall invented the "whaleback" steamer.
Steamer *City of Detroit II* built for the D & C Lines.

1890—Lake sailing ship era on the wane.
Merritt Brothers opened first ore mine on the Mesabi Range; later to become the largest and greatest of the world's producing iron districts.

THE PARADE OF THE YEARS

1891—Devils Island Lighthouse (Apostle Islands) in Lake Superior established.
First lake steamer crossed the Atlantic.

1892—First Great Lakes carferry started on Lake Michigan.
Electric trolley patented.

1893—Chicago World's Fair held.
Steamer *Christopher Columbus,* only whaleback passenger ship built, entered service out of Chicago.

1894—Palatial steamer *North West* built; latest word in luxury, speed and design; operated between Buffalo and Duluth.

1895—Steamer *North Land,* sister ship of the *North West,* built.
Canadian lock at the Soo opened to navigation.
Steamer *Chicora* sank in Lake Michigan—26 lives lost.
Lumber hauling on the lakes diminishes.

1896—Poe Lock at the Soo opened. Then the largest lock in the world.
Steamer *City of Buffalo* built for the Cleveland & Buffalo Line.

1897—Steamer *City of Erie* built for the Cleveland & Buffalo Line.

1898—Spanish-American War. Duration 3½ months.
Freighter *Superior City* launched, largest vessel then on the lakes.

1899—The Pittsburgh Steamship Company organized.

The American Shipbuilding Company organized.

1900—Electric lights began to appear on lake ships.

1901—The "big race" between steamers *Tashmoo* and *City of Erie* on Lake Erie.
First wireless telegraph across the Atlantic.

1902—Whaleback steamer *Thomas Wilson* sank near Duluth in collision with steamer *George Hadley*— 9 lives lost.

1903—Steamer *James H. Hoyt* built. First ship on lakes with hatches spaced on 12 foot centers. Wright Brothers first successful aeroplane flight at Kitty Hawk, N. C.

1904—Passenger steamer *Juniata* launched at Cleveland. Marine tragedy near New York City. Excursion steamer *General Slocum* burned—1,021 lives lost.

1905—Freighter *Mataafa* wrecked within sight of Duluth —9 lives lost. *Mataafa* afterward salvaged and returned to service.

1906—Steamers *E. Y. Townsend* and *D. J. Morrell* built. Early six-hundred footers.

1908—First self-unloading bulk carrier appeared. Freighter *D. M. Clemson* sank in Lake Superior— 24 lives lost.

1909—Freighter *Shenango* built. Early 600 footer. First iron smelted by electricity.
Steamer *Russia* foundered in Lake Huron—13 lives lost.
Steamer *Tempest No. 2* burned in Georgian Bay— 6 lives lost.

Steamer *Badger State* burned in Lake Huron—15 lives lost.

Steamer *Clarion* burned in Lake Erie — 32 lives lost.

Carferry *Marquette & Bessemer No. 2* disappeared in Lake Erie—36 lives lost.

1910—Split Rock lighthouse built on Lake Superior. Passenger steamer *Octorara* launched at Wyandotte, Mich.

1911—Palatial passenger steamer *North West* burned at Buffalo dock.
Separate sailing courses laid out on Lake Huron for up and down bound ships to prevent accidents.
Tug *Silver Spray* sank off Cleveland—9 lives lost.

1912—Lake passenger liner *Seeandbee* launched for the C & B Line, largest and finest passenger ship then on the lakes.
Titanic sank in Atlantic on maiden voyage Liverpool to New York—1,513 lives lost.

1913—The "Big Storm." Freighters lost or wrecked were: *Henry B. Smith, Isaac M. Scott, John A. McGean, Argus, Hydrus, Charles S. Price, James Carruthers, Leafield, Wm. Nottingham, Regina, Wexford, L. C. Waldo, Howard M. Hanna* and *Lightship No. 82.*

1914—Start of the World War I in Europe.
Davis Lock at the Soo opened.
Panama Canal opened to navigation.
Steamer *C. F. Curtis* with barges *Marvin* and *Peterson* in tow disappeared near Grand Marais, Mich.—26 lives lost.

1915—Excursion steamer *Eastland* overturned at Chicago—812 lives lost.

Lusitania torpedoed and sunk, bound from New York to Liverpool—1,198 lives lost.

First radio across the Atlantic.

First telephone across the United States.

Veteran freighter *Onoko* foundered in Lake Superior.

1916—"Black Friday" storm on Lake Erie. Freighters lost or wrecked were: *Merida, Marshall F. Butters* and the *James B. Colgate* and the schooner *D. L. Filer.*

United States Shipping Board created.

1917—United States entered World War I. (April 6th.)

1918—French mine sweepers *Cerisoler* and *Inkerman* disappeared in Lake Superior—76 lost. No trace of them was ever found.

Armistice signed ending World War I hostilities. (Nov. 11th.)

1919—Sabin Lock at the Soo opened to navigation. Freighters *Myron, H. E. Runnels* and *John Owen* sank in a wind storm on the upper lakes—40 lives lost.

1920—Steamer *Superior City* sank in Lake Superior when in collision a boiler exploded—29 lives lost.

1921—Palatial passenger steamer *North Land* scrapped on St. Lawrence River.

1922—Tug *Cornell* lost between Cleveland and Buffalo—8 lives lost.

1923—Old *U. S. S. Wolverine* ended her sailing days.

Engine trouble developed which was never repaired.

1924—Old passenger steamer *State of Ohio* burned at C & B Line dock in Cleveland.

Whaleback *Clifton* sank in Lake Huron—28 lives lost.

Wooden freighter *Orinoco* sank in Lake Huron—4 lives lost.

1925—Sandsucker *Kelley Island* sank in Lake Erie—9 lives lost. Later was salvaged and returned to service.

1927—Steamer *Kamloops* disappeared in Lake Superior with 22 men in a winter blow.

Steamer *Harry L. Coulby* launched for the Interlake Steamship Co.; outstanding ship in size and appointments.

Peace Bridge over Niagara River opened for traffic and dedicated by the Prince of Wales.

Lindbergh flew alone across the Atlantic.

First telephone across the Atlantic.

Television first demonstrated.

1929—Grand Trunk carferry *Milwaukee* plunged to the bottom of Lake Michigan with her crew of 52.

Steamer *Wisconsin* sank in Lake Michigan — 16 lives lost.

Steamer *Chicago* wrecked on Michipicoten Island in Lake Superior, but her crew were rescued after several days.

Steamer *Andaste* foundered in Lake Michigan—25 lives lost.

Ambassador Bridge over Detroit River opened to traffic.

1930—Steamer *George J. Whelan* foundered off Dunkirk in Lake Erie—15 lives lost.

1932—Steamer *John J. Boland, Jr.,* foundered off Barcelona, N. Y., in Lake Erie—4 lives lost.

1933—Bank holiday and financial chaos.

1934—Passenger ship *Morro Castle* burned off New Jersey in Atlantic—124 lives lost.

1935—Passenger steamer *Tashmoo* wrecked in Detroit River, no lives lost.

1936—Sandsucker *Material Service* sank off Chicago—15 lives lost.
Sandsucker *Sand Merchant* sank off Cleveland—19 lives lost.

1937—Steamers *Governor Miller, William A. Irvin, John Hulst* and *Ralph H. Watson* built for the Pittsburgh Steamship Company.
Passenger steamers *Octorara, Juniata* and *Tionesta* withdrawn from service.

1938—C. & B. Line steamer *City of Buffalo* burned at her dock in Cleveland.
Detroit and Windsor ferries suspended service.

1939—U. S. Coast Guard and the Lighthouse Service combined.
Blue Water Bridge between Port Huron, Mich., and Sarnia, Ont., opened to traffic.
Diving bell first used in submarine rescue work.
War again in Europe. (Sept. 3rd.)

1940—Canadian steamer *Arlington* sank during a severe wind and snow storm on Lake Superior on May 1st. Crew of 16 rescued by steamer *Collingwood* but Captain Fred Burke went down with his ship.

⚓ ⚓ ⚓ ⚓ ⚓ ⚓ ⚓ ⚓

CHAPTER TWO

DID YOU KNOW THAT . . . ?

. . . . The most southerly port on the Great Lakes is Huron, Ohio. It is a little toward the south of midway between latitudes 41 and 42.

. . . . The most westerly port on the Great Lakes is Duluth, Minn. It is just west of 92 longitude.

. . . . The most easterly port on the Great Lakes is Sackett's Harbor, N. Y. It is just east of 76 longitude.

. . . . The most northerly port on the Great Lakes is Nipigon, Ontario. It is just north of latitude 49.

. . . . The deepest water on the Great Lakes is in Lake Superior, being about 1,300 feet.

. . . . Darkness commences below 200 feet and below 350 feet the water is inky black.

. . . . Small light draft boats can get from the Great Lakes to the Mississippi River by two different routes: One, via Chicago and the Illinois Canal; and the other, via Green Bay and the Fox River.

. . . . Fairly large ships can reach New York City and tidewater from the Great Lakes via the New York State Barge Canal which runs from Buffalo, N. Y., to Albany, N. Y., on the Hudson River; thence down that river to New York City and tidewater.

. . . . Ocean boats can enter the Great Lakes via the St. Lawrence River through which a series of canal locks brings them around rapids and shoal water. The Welland Canal carries the ships between Lakes Ontario and

Erie, around Niagara Falls.   The Soo Canal lifts them between Lakes Huron and Superior in the St. Mary's River, around the shoal water and rapids of that stream.

. . . . Lake Superior is the largest body of fresh water in the world, having 31,200 square miles of water surface. Lake Huron is the second largest lake of the Great Lakes, having 23,800 square miles of water surface, this includes Georgian Bay, which is adjoining.   Lake Michigan has 22,450 square miles of water surface.   Lake Erie has 9,960 square miles of water surface, while Lake Ontario is the smallest in water surface of all the five Great Lakes, having 7,240 square miles.   Connecting waters have the following water surfaces: St. Mary's River, 150 square miles; St. Clair River, 25 square miles; Lake St. Clair, 410 square miles; Detroit River, 25 square miles; Niagara River, 15 square miles.

. . . . The number of feet above sea level of each of the Great Lakes is as follows: Lake Superior—602 feet; Lake Michigan and Lake Huron—581 feet; Lake Erie—573 feet; Lake Ontario—247 feet.

. . . . Lake Michigan is the only one of the five Great Lakes that lies entirely within the borders of the United States.

. . . . The annual movement of bulk freight, including all traffic on the Great Lakes, averages about 100 million net tons, but reached a maximum of 160 million tons in 1929.   The combined annual movement of cargo freight through the Panama, Suez, Manchester and Kiel Canals for the 15 years, 1920 to 1934 inclusive, averaged 70 million tons.   The lakes movement was accomplished in the approximate seven and one-half month navigation season, while the other canals are open the entire year.

. . . . The government spent on the improvement of the St. Mary's River, a total of about 27 million dollars. This included all the locks, entrance channels and river improvements. The Panama Canal cost about 378 million dollars, without fortifications, or about fourteen times that spent on the Soo improvements. The Suez Canal cost 140 million dollars, or over five times the Soo. The New York Barge Canal cost 150 million dollars; the Manchester Ship Canal in England, 75 million dollars. The cost of the Soo locks and canal is small in comparison with the other large important waterways of the world, but there is none equal to it in the traffic carried. The locks are free of toll charges to any vessel in the world.

. . . . One third of the population of the United States find their occupation and their homes in the states that border on the lakes. Much of this occupation arose in one manner or another because of the lakes, and much of it still survives because of them.

. . . . You can navigate by your watch! Point the hour hand at the sun and due south will lie exactly midway between the hour hand and the figure 12 on the dial. For example: if it is nine o'clock, you point the hour hand at the sun and then due south will be just between the 10 and 11.

. . . . Sandusky was once known as Ogontz, named for a converted Indian who had a cabin on what is now Market Street about a block east of Columbus Avenue.

. . . . Early explorers gave Sandusky Bay its name—Lac Sandouski, meaning Cold Water Lake. French trading posts flourished and the Lilies of France flew over the territory until 1762, when the British banner went up, to remain exactly fourteen years.

. . . . Pontiac, the great Indian chief, was a regular traveler across Sandusky Bay.

. . . . In 1832, when Sandusky had some thirty houses, the village undertook to finance and build the second railroad west of the Allegheny Mountains. By dint of hard work, much oratory and a glowing prospectus, more than a million dollars was raised in northern and western Ohio and the Mad River and Lake Erie Railroad was commenced. Eventually this road ran from Sandusky to Springfield, Ohio. It is still in use, being now a part of the Baltimore and Ohio system.

. . . . The Great Lakes are nearly 100,000 square miles in size. It is 2,200 miles from the head of Lake Superior to tidewater in the Gulf of Saint Lawrence.

. . . . Lake Erie is the oldest of the Great Lakes, say geologists, and the shallowest. It is the eleventh biggest body of fresh water in the world.

. . . . The word "Erie" is a corruption of the Iroquois Indian word "Erige," meaning cat or panther. Early French maps call Lake Erie "Lac Du Chat"—Lake of the Cat. The Erie Indians, who once controlled the southern shore of Lake Erie, were fierce, arrogant and proud of their name—"People of the Cats." In 1645, because they lost an athletic contest with the Iroquois, they began a war which eventually ended with the complete destruction of the Cat People.

DID YOU KNOW THAT . . . ?

. . . . Displacement is the weight of a ship, determined by the amount of water it displaces.

. . . . The gross tonnage of a ship is the cubical measurements of all enclosed spaces. The gross tonnage is found by dividing by 100 the whole interior capacity—expressed in cubic feet—of the hull of a ship and her enclosed deck houses. This method presumes that an average cargo of light-weight freight would require approximately 100 cubic feet for every ton of actual weight.

. . . . One half of all the fresh water in the world is in the Great Lakes.

. . . . The total length of shore line of the Great Lakes and connecting rivers down to St. Regis, N. Y., where the St. Lawrence ceases to be the International Boundary, is 8,117 miles, of which 3,774 are in Canada, and the balance, 4,343 are in the United States.

. . . . The State of Michigan has the longest shore line of any state in the United States bordering on the Great Lakes. It has 2,389 miles of shore line, which is more than half of the entire Great Lakes' shore line in the United States. Michigan shores are washed by all but one of the Great Lakes.

. . . . When Eliza of "Uncle Tom's Cabin" crossed the ice floes of the Ohio River it is supposed that she was Sandusky bound. Thousands of escaping slaves before her had traveled this same route. Sandusky was the northern terminus of the famed "Underground Railroad" along which escaping slaves were hurried to Canada and freedom. So efficient was the "Underground" that it boasted of 100% success.

. . . . During November 1928 the amazing total of

almost 108½ million bushels of wheat passed down through the Sault Locks. The largest wheat movement through the Panama Canal for an entire year amounted to 113,389,669 bushels.

. . . . To a captain on the Great Lakes, story has it, should go the credit of the word "stateroom" as applied to ships. He conceived the idea of dividing the deck into individual rooms so that families could occupy them, and he designated such rooms with the names of states. Hence came the word "stateroom." The largest room aboard was named Texas, after the largest state. The crew used this room. Today the crew's quarters aft of the pilot house is still known as "the texas."

. . . . The port of Duluth is second in tonnage to New York. Duluth has the world's greatest iron ore fields at its back door.

. . . . The distance, on the vessel course, from tidewater at Montreal to the head of the Great Lakes at Duluth, is 1,346 miles.

. . . . Years ago ships told the time by ringing the bell. The day was divided into six watches of four hours each, beginning at midnight. The end of the first half-hour of a watch was announced by one stroke of the ship's bell. Another stroke was rung for each succeeding half hour, until eight bells was struck. The strokes were rung in pairs. Eight bells was reached at 4, 8, and 12 o'clock, which marked the end of each watch.

. . . . When two vessels approach each other on the Great Lakes, one blast of the ship's whistle means, "I am directing my course to starboard."

DID YOU KNOW THAT . . . ?

. . . . Two blasts of the ship's whistle means, "I am directing my course to port."

. . . . Standing amidships facing forward, to your right is starboard, and to your left is port.

. . . . Canada is south of the United States—it is at a point at Belle Isle in Detroit, where the Detroit River boundary twists peculiarly, bringing this about.

. . . . Before ships pass each other, either meeting or overtaking, where the passing is to be close, both ships must agree as to the passing by their whistle signals before actually passing each other.

. . . . Whenever there is thick weather by reason of fog, mist, falling snow, heavy rainstorms, or other causes, whether by night or day, fog signals are blown on the ship's whistle. Usually these are three short blasts with not more than one minute intervals between each series of three blasts.

. . . . Ships carry sidelights located well forward and well up in height, usually near their pilot houses. The sidelight on the starboard side is green, and the one on the port side is red. This tells navigators at night which way another ship is headed. When both red and green lights can be seen, it tells that the other ship is headed directly at that point.

. . . The signals rung on a bell or blown on an engine-room whistle by the navigating officer from the ship's bridge to the engineer in the engine-room are as follows:

1 whistle or 1 bell. . . . . Go Ahead
1 whistle or 1 bell. . . . . Stop
2 whistles or 2 bells. . . . . Back

3 whistles or 3 bells...................Check
4 whistles or 4 bells...................Strong
4 whistles or 4 bells...................All Right

. . . . When two steamers are meeting in narrow channels, such as the Detroit River, St. Clair River, and St. Mary's River, the down bound, or descending steamer has the right of way, and usually signals first.

. . . . The "long ton", so generally used in the lake bulk trade, is of 2,240 pounds, rather than the commercial avoirdupois ton of 2,000 pounds.

. . . . A big lake freighter can carry nearly a half million bushels of wheat. It requires approximately 22,000 acres of farm land to produce such a cargo. When the railroads bring it to the ship's dock, it requires about 30 trains of 65 cars to haul it overland. If baked into bread it would make about 4,500,000 loaves.

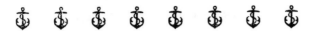

Chapter Three

THE GRIFFIN

In a small clearing in the dense wilderness on the east bank of the Niagara River at a point where the Cayuga Creek empties into it, was built the first ship ever to make a voyage on the Great Lakes. A band of hardy explorers and adventurers, mostly Frenchmen, under the leadership of Rene Robert Cavalier, Sieur de la Salle, known today as La Salle, together with the intrepid priest, Father Hennepin, cut the trees of the forest and fashioned for themselves a ship with which to sail out upon these all but unknown waters. This was in the winter of 1679. Sixty-four years earlier, Champlain had first discovered the Great Lakes. Jean Nicolet had explored the Les Cheneaux Islands near Mackinac in 1634. Father Marquette had founded a mission at the Soo in 1668. Lake Erie was first sighted by the white man in 1669. La Salle came early to this wild country.

La Salle had built a small ship on the shores of Lake Ontario before he started work on the *Griffin,* but the ship had been soon lost. He now wanted to sail the upper lakes above the falls at Niagara, and so it was that he cleared the site mentioned and laid the keel for his *Griffin.* The exact spot is now said to be the town of La Salle, New York, between Niagara Falls and Black Rock.

31

Throughout the winter the men labored constructing the ship. When spring came to the forest, and the ice thawed, they had their boat ready to launch into the water. A tiny ship of from forty-five to sixty tons burden, she was duly christened the *Griffin,* sometimes spelled *Griffon* and *Le Griffon.* She was outfitted crudely for her proposed journey into the upper lakes. It was intended that she should go for furs, to be bartered from the Indians along the shores, and eventually to be marketed in the European export trade.

On August seventh, the *Griffin* started on her voyage with thirty-four men aboard, sailing up the Niagara River and out onto the broad waters of Lake Erie. Astonished Indians lined the shore to watch "the great white bird" spread its wings and glide gracefully away.

La Salle's party crossed Lake Erie in three days and then anchored at the mouth of what is now the Detroit River. Fresh bear meat and other wild game were loaded aboard the *Griffin* and the voyage up the river was continued.

Father Hennepin wrote of the voyage and it is his writings that today tell us of the dreams and difficulties encountered by these early lake sailors. He named the body of water at the head of the Detroit River, Lake St. Claire, and the river emptying into it he called by the same name. These were so named, because it was the day of the Festival of Saint Claire, on their calendar, when they arrived.

All went well aboard the tiny sailboat and soon she was out on the swelling waters of Lake Huron. Fate here took a hand and engulfed the *Griffin* in one of those savage summer storms which occasionally sweep that section. The crew became terrified and blamed their leader La Salle for their plight. Hennepin sought to calm them. Fortunately, the storm did not last long and soon the huge waves flattened and the *Griffin* ceased to pitch and roll.

Onward she then sailed until she entered what is now the Straits of Mackinac. Here, at Saint Ignace de Michillimackinack, they rested awhile at the Jesuit Mission. Then onward again the little ship sailed and on September third, entered Lake Michigan, then called by the Indians, "Illinois." Her memorable trip ended when she anchored in what is now Green Bay. Here La Salle found a great abundance of valuable furs. Anxious for funds to finance his explorations and being at the time hard pressed by his creditors, La Salle hastened to load his cockleshell with a full cargo of the furs.

Against the advice of many of his followers, La Salle decided to send the *Griffin* back down the lakes to dispose of the cargo and satisfy his creditors. It was planned that the *Griffin* should return the following spring to Lake Michigan and pick up the party that would remain and explore the wilderness. La Salle decided to remain at the head of this group and continue his explorations. Thus it was that, on September 18th, with her pilot and five sailors, the *Griffin* weighed anchor, bid farewell to La Salle, Father Hennepin and their men, and spread her sails for Lake Erie. This was the last ever seen of the *Griffin*.

That night a gale swept the lake and continued to blow for several days. It is believed that the *Griffin* perished with all hands in this storm. Some think her crew turned traitor and landed, sold the cargo, scuttled the ship, and went inland, only to be killed by the Indians. Whatever occurred, the fact remains that the ship never made port.

Occasionally, during the past few years, it has been reported that the wreck of the *Griffin* has been located. Men digging on the shores near where it is thought the *Griffin* went down, have found buried in the sands, the stout oak timbers of bygone ships. Whether it was actually the wreck of the *Griffin* or not, will of course, never be known. Many ships of wood have perished on these lakes in the years since the *Griffin* was lost, and the bones of one are much like those of another. Nothing remains but words to tell of the ill-fated cruise of the gallant little fur trader.

CHAPTER FOUR

THE UNITED STATES BRIG NIAGARA

Few persons, among the millions living today within a radius of several hundred miles of Put-in-Bay, Ohio, which is located on South Bass Island in Lake Erie, have ever given the Battle of Lake Erie much thought. But were it not for the United States victory in this battle, these same millions in this territory would, very likely at present, be living under British rule, and the entire Great Lakes would be "the King's Inland Waterway."

During the War of 1812, Great Britain and the United States were battling each other for the freedom of the seas, and incidentally for supremacy and territory in the New World.

Several gallant victories were won by United States sailors in heavy fighting on the high seas, but let us focus our attention on the Great Lakes area. Here we find that, early in the war, Fort Dearborn at Detroit, had been evacuated by the United States troops and the River Raisin Indian Massacre had occurred, leaving the district of Detroit and Southern Michigan under British control. Indians harassed the settlers and confusion reigned. Fort Mackinac also fell to the British during the summer of 1812. Because of this and other British minor victories, the new republic was hard pressed to save its Great Lakes territory.

Then, in what appeared to be the darkest hour of the war, young Commodore Oliver Hazard Perry, at that time only twenty-eight years old, abandoned his bloody and crippled ship, the *Lawrence,* during the Battle of Lake Erie, which was fought near Put-In-Bay on September 10, 1813. He transferred his remaining crew to the waiting *Niagara,* and, with a Heaven-sent breeze, sailed her between the British main fleet, splitting their battleground in two. By valiant gunfire from both sides of his *Niagara,* he subdued the enemy's fleet. The fighting lasted three hours and fifteen minutes, and ended after forty-one were killed and ninety-four wounded among the British, and thirty killed and ninety-three wounded among the Americans. The British never afterward attempted to do battle for this territory. The Lakes had been saved for the United States, and the *Niagara* did the job!

It was then that Perry wrote his famous dispatch to General Harrison, that has since been a by-word, "We have met the enemy and they are ours; two ships; two brigs; one schooner and one sloop." In a postscript he added, "Send us some soldiers to help take care of the prisoners, who are more numerous than ourselves."

What was this ship *Niagara* that had saved the day, and whence came it? Its story is interesting.

Captain Daniel Dobbins appears to have been the first man to cause actual work to be started on building the *Niagara.* He, then a resident of Erie, Pennsylvania, informed President Madison and other government heads at Washington of the precarious situation existing in the Great Lakes frontier country. He was promptly authorized to build a battle fleet to protect that territory.

In the autumn of 1812 work was started at Erie on six vessels of what was to be Perry's fleet of nine. These six were the *Lawrence, Niagara, Ariel, Scorpion, Tigress* and *Porcupine.* The first three mentioned were built at the mouth of Cascade Creek, where it enters Erie Bay on Lake Erie, the balance being built at Lee's Creek, also on Erie Bay. The vessels *Caledonia, Somers* and *Trippe* were later acquired and completed the Perry squadron.

Captain Dobbins brought professional ship builders of the famous salt water Yankee frigate ships from the eastern sea coast to construct the new lake fleet. The new ships were modeled and hewn into shape by hand, of selected trees from the forests around Erie. Great care was taken to procure sturdy, tough wood which would withstand gunshelling and the abuses of battle. The *Niagara* was one hundred eighteen feet in length, thirty feet beam and about nine feet draft. The fleet was built along salt water lines, but corrected for shallow water sailing, which was necessary in Lake Erie.

Oliver Hazard Perry came to Erie in March of 1813 and proceeded at once to complete and outfit the new fleet for battle action. On August 12, 1813, the fleet sailed out of Erie in search of the British squadron which then had complete control of Lake Erie and was under the command of Commodore Robert H. Barclay.

The two opposing battle fleets met near Put-In-Bay about noon on the tenth of September, that year, and the bloody conflict and the American victory, previously mentioned, occurred. Perry then returned to Erie, arriving there about one month from the day he had first sailed, bringing with him his prisoners of war and their ships; the *Lady Prevost, Chippewa, Detroit, Queen Charlotte, General Hunter* and *Little Belt.*

Commodore Perry was hailed as a national hero and his fame still rings throughout the land. He eventually returned to his home in Newport, Rhode Island, but continued in the government service. It was while on such work in Trinidad, South America, on August 23, 1819, his thirty-second birthday, that he died of yellow fever. His body was buried there but was later removed to the United States and reburied in 'the cemetery at Newport, Rhode Island.

The vessels of the battle fleets, both victors and vanquished, lay anchored in a small bay off the larger Bay of Erie. It was here that the survivors were called upon to wage another battle, this one against the elements and disease. The following winter was terribly severe and their suffering intense. Disease spread through the crews and many died and were buried on the shore nearby. The small bay in which they were anchored grew to be called Misery Bay, and the burial plot was called Graveyard Pond. These names have come down through the years, being known locally as such today.

Commercial shipping, which, after the war, was fast growing on the lakes, took over the most adaptable of the war vessels anchored in Misery Bay. The *Lady Prevost* and the *Queen Charlotte* had many years of later service in the peaceful merchant shipping service, and several of the others served the same purpose. Those not so adaptable to refitting for commercial sailing were left to rot and eventually sink. The *Niagara* was one of the latter. She was left to rest for about eighty years on the bottom of the bay before anyone took further notice of her.

The public became interested in the old vessel when the one hundredth anniversary of Perry's Victory was to be celebrated, and looked around for ways and means to refloat the old brig and outfit her if possible as she was at the time of the battle. The Pennsylvania Perry's Victory Centennial Commission was formed, and, under the expert guidance of Captain William L. Morrison, then commanding the *U. S. S. Wolverine* on the Great Lakes, the work of raising the sunken vessel was ordered. Funds were authorized to cover the expenses by the State Legislature of Pennsylvania.

The *Niagara* lay under twenty feet of water and six feet of sand. Contracts for raising her were let on November 10, 1912, and on March 6, 1913, she was brought above the heavy ice that then coated Misery Bay. Her upper works and cabins were gone, but about two-thirds of the hull was still in fair condition and on her port side the old gun ports still showed. Her keel, stem, some timbers and some planking were in such condition as to be usable in her rebuilding. She was carefully "cradled" to the shore of Presque Isle where the work of restoring her to her original self was started. Several old bayonets, axe heads and round shot were brought up with the *Niagara* in her hold when she was raised, and are now in the possession of various historical societies.

Under the careful supervision of Captain Morrison all the details of the old ship were preserved. Her original lines were strictly adhered to:—the sailing spar plan; the old cannons she carried; everything was carefully restored to its original order.

On June 7, 1913, she was launched into Erie Bay for the second time. She grounded before getting into deep water and tugs pulled on her for several hours before she was finally dragged into deep water again. A patriotic launching party assembled at the ways, and many interesting historical talks were given by famous men and women of that day. The *Niagara* was towed to the Public Dock at Erie and outfitted for her great Perry Victory Centennial cruise up and down the Great Lakes.

This cruise started about the middle of July, 1913, from Erie. The rebuilt *Niagara* looked exactly as she did when sailed by Commodore Perry one hundred years previous, only this time it was convoyed by the *United States Ship Wolverine*. The cruise was under the command of Captain Morrison, who acted as captain for both vessels.

Millions of persons saw and went aboard the old ship in her visits to Fairport, Cleveland, Sandusky, Put-In-Bay, Monroe, Toledo, Detroit, Green Bay, Milwaukee, Chicago and Buffalo. Much interest was developed in lake history and shipping on this cruise.

The *Niagara* was returned to Erie after the Perry Centennial cruise and docked at the Public Dock there. Time kept up its never ceasing work of destruction, and the partly old and partly new *Niagara* began to show the consequent effects. By the summer of 1932 she was again in bad condition, her planking seams opening and generally rotting throughout. She could not be trusted to float even across Erie Bay. Captain Morrison still watched over the rotting brig, and with the help of finances from the State of Pennsylvania, he arranged to again have her restored.

The *Niagara* was placed bodily on a large scow and carried across Erie Bay to the shore of the peninsula, which is now Presque Isle State Park. There she was placed on the beach where the work of taking apart the once rebuilt ship, and, for the third time, of building her, was commenced.

Only the keel of the original *Niagara*, a stout timber of black oak, fourteen by eighteen inches, was fit for use in the restoration of the old ship. But around this original backbone was to be built again the same *Niagara* as it was in those wild days of 1813 when she sailed into the British fleet, and saved the Great Lakes Country for the United States. It was intended she should be a floating museum of historical lore of the days when ships of her type conquered and ruled the world.

Unfortunately, lack of funds halted the work of restoration. Today the partially rebuilt *Niagara* stands on the ways by the water's edge, deserted by all. It is to be hoped that ways and means will soon be found to complete this work of restoration of the historic old *Niagara* for posterity.

Note: As this book goes to print, the work of restoration of the Niagara is again proceeding. Workmen are busy with hammer and saw. It is reported that the Pennsylvania Historical Society has obtained government funds with which to carry on the work.

⚓ ⚓ ⚓ ⚓ ⚓ ⚓ ⚓ ⚓

Chapter Five

THE WALK · IN · THE · WATER

At Black Rock, New York, near Buffalo, was constructed the first steamboat to ply Lake Erie and the upper lakes. Two earlier steamers, the *Frontenac*, a Canadian trader, and the *Ontario*, an American vessel, had been built and operated on Lake Ontario during the years 1816 and 1817. These are the first two steamboats to be recorded on the Great Lakes. A haphazard sidewheeler called the *Accommodation* is reported as having operated on the Saint Lawrence River between Montreal and Quebec in 1809, some few years prior to the building of the *Frontenac* and the *Ontario*.

The steamboat built at Black Rock, mentioned above, was named *"Walk-in-the-Water,"* so named from a remark of an Indian that had seen Robert Fulton's *Clermont* operate on the Hudson River. The *Walk-in-the-Water* was built as a passenger and freight carrier, and was launched on May 28, 1818. Noah Brown, a shipbuilder of New York City, supervised her construction. Robert Fulton directed the power installation. In August, 1807, Fulton had made his famous run in his *Clermont* on the Hudson River, the first generally accepted steamboat trip.

Steamboat building on the lakes kept pace with this type of construction on the Atlantic; in fact the lakes were a little ahead of the salt water. It was in 1819, a year after the *Walk-in-the-Water* was launched, that the American steamboat *City of Savannah,* described as a "full-rigged ship with steam paddles," sailed from Savannah to Liverpool. However, she used her engines for only a small portion of the entire voyage, having exhausted her supply of wood fuel. On April 22, 1838, the British steamer *Sirius* dropped anchor in New York Harbor, bringing ninety-four passengers from Liverpool. A single day later another British steamboat, the *Great Western,* arrived. Thus trans-Atlantic steamer passenger service began with a race, or almost a race. The *Great Western* had hoped to overtake the *Sirius* and, although larger and faster, she did not quite make it. Today, a century later, the race to make the best time across the North Atlantic still continues.

The *Sirius* and *Great Western* and their immediate successors used steam as their primary power. They carried sails, as did practically all steamers until later years of the nineteenth century. As these boats made nine or ten knots it required about fourteen days to complete a crossing. The windjamming Yankee clipper ships often made faster time.

But to return to freshwater, after the *Walk-in-the-Water* was launched into the Niagara River, it was found that her power was insufficient to propel her against the fast running current to get her into Lake Erie. Auxiliary power in the form of twenty yoke of the humble oxen were supplied. With ropes attached to the new steamer these beasts of burden walked the tow path that led to the lake. Thus it was that the first steamer entered Lake Erie. This oxen towing was dubbed "a horn breeze" by the wags of the river-front, and was a regular procedure for all craft in those days.

The *Walk-in-the-Water* was a cross between a steamer and a sailing craft. She carried two high masts and was fitted with a square rigged foresail. Her new-fangled smoke stack stood between the masts amidships. Two large paddle boxes which housed her paddle wheels were placed exactly amidships and protruded clumsily from her deck. She was about one hundred fifty feet in overall length, and thirty feet beam, and had an eight foot depth. Her gross tonnage was three hundred thirty-eight tons. Her bow was high, as was her stern, similar to her sailing ship sisters, and she proudly displayed on her bows a carved figurehead of Commodore Oliver Hazard Perry.

Her passenger quarters were all below deck. The women's cabin was partitioned off in the forward part of the boat. Then followed the men's quarters, then the small dining room, and lastly the tiny smoking room adjoining the baggage room.

The steam whistle had not yet been invented. This event occurred in 1843. Therefore the *Walk-in-the-Water* boasted of a small cannon mounted on her forward deck, which was used to signal the ship's intentions. It was always fired just before she docked to inform the inhabitants of the port of her arrival. A farewell shot was customarily fired upon her departure.

Her first trip was to Detroit, stopping at Dunkirk, Erie and Cleveland enroute. It was a momentous occasion.

THE WALK-IN-THE-WATER

Captain Job Fish, a Hudson River boatman, regaled in a new uniform with much decoration, stood upon the crest of the paddle box and directed and signaled his engineer until the *Walk-in-the-Water* was well out on Lake Erie. All local activity at the ports of call was transferred to the water front as the new contraption appeared on the horizon. The voyage, commencing at Black Rock, started on August 23, 1818. Twenty-nine fare-paying passengers were aboard. It cost them for cabin fare: eight dollars to Erie; fifteen dollars to Cleveland; twenty-four dollars to Detroit.

With wood smoke and hot sparks pouring spasmodically from her stack at each asthmatic wheeze of the engine, she puffed her way into and out of each harbor. Many of the spectators were Indians, who quaked in the knees at the majestic and fearful spectacle before them. Nightfall of the twenty-fifth found the *Walk-in-the-Water* at the mouth of the Detroit River. Here, as was the custom, the ship awaited daybreak before attempting to navigate the river.

Detroit had prepared excitedly for the new steamboat's arrival. Judge Augustus B. Woodward and many other prominent Detroiters went down the river to board the steamer that they might be on deck when she arrived in Detroit. The new Hudson's Wharf had just been built at the foot of Bates Street to accommodate the new steamboat. Villagers crowded the dock and river banks long before the boat appeared, each trying to catch the first glimpse.

"Boom!" thundered the ship's cannon as the *Walk-in-*

the-Water appeared around a curve in the river. All Detroit was now on hand as a reception committee. After considerable difficulty and much loud shouting, the *Walk-in-the-Water* was made fast to the wharf. Thus on the morning of August 26th, 1818, did the first steamer arrive at Detroit. It had required forty-four hours and ten minutes traveling time to make the trip. Today the giant lake liners make the trip in fifteen hours.

The *Walk-in-the-Water* continued to make her trips between Buffalo and Detroit. Captain Fish evidently tired of the strenuous lake sailor life and returned to the more tranquil Hudson River.

During June, 1820, the little steamer ventured far to the northward, crossing the length of Lake Huron and landing at Mackinac Island, where she discharged her passengers, a troop of United States soldiers. Again in August of the same year she steamed to Mackinac, this time with passengers on pleasure bent. Her crowning cruise was made in 1821 when she triumphantly puffed all the way from Buffalo to Detroit, Mackinac and into Green Bay, off Lake Michigan. She made this cruise, one way, in eight days, which considering all things, was a very good showing for the little beginner. This gave her an average cruising speed of some six or seven miles per hour.

Business continued good for the new venture, and this fact probably caused its untimely end. The *Walk-in-the-Water* was operating on Lake Erie a bit too late in the season of 1821. On the last day of October of that year, loaded at Black Rock with passengers and a small amount of freight, she cleared that port at four in the afternoon bound for Cleveland and Detroit. She had barely passed Buffalo when a violent gale suddenly blew across Lake Erie and caught the *Walk-in-the-Water* in all its fury. Captain Jedediah Rogers is reported to have been in charge of the ship at the time.

He had turned his ship around and headed back for Buffalo at eight o'clock that night, when he learned that the water was entering the hull, through opening seams in her planking, faster than her pumps could remove it. Not being able to reach port, he decided to anchor and attempt to ride out the gale. Three anchors were hove over, one held by a chain and the other two by ropes. A terrible night of horror was spent by all on board, as all hands struggled to keep the ship afloat.

At ten that night one anchor rope broke, and by midnight the other rope snapped. The remaining chained anchor could not hold the ship in the gale and, as good fortune would have it, she slowly dragged toward the beach instead of the open water. At four-thirty the next morning, November first, her bottom scraped the sands of the shore, near Point Abino not far from Buffalo. As daylight came, the gale subsided and a line was hauled ashore and made fast to a stout tree. By the help of this line the ship's life boat was able to transfer all the passengers and crew safely ashore without the loss of a single life. Thus ended the first steamer of the upper Great Lakes, a wreck.

Due to her position as she grounded, and the nearness to her home port, it was possible to rescue all of her fur-

47

niture, fixtures and engines. The engines were reconditioned and were installed in another steamboat, the *Superior,* which was built as soon as possible.

These engines served to propel the *Superior* until she also met the fate of the *Walk-in-the-Water,* a wreck. Once again the engines were salvaged and placed aboard the ship *Charles Townsend,* where they served for many years. They were finally removed from this latter ship and oddly enough, the main cylinder of this already old engine is said to have served as a blowing cylinder ashore in an engine works in Buffalo. It is reported that this cylinder was still in daily use as late as 1902 in this capacity.

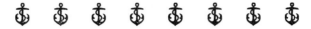

Chapter Six

THE WOLVERINE

Thirty years after Commodore Oliver Hazard Perry's famous battle of Lake Erie, in which the historic *Niagara* took so prominent a part, there was launched at Erie, Pennsylvania, the *United States Ship Michigan,* now the *Wolverine.* Those thirty years covered what is probably the era of the most revolutionary transition from old to new in ship construction, the *Niagara* representing the wooden ship of sailing days, and the *Michigan,* the modern steamer of today.

Through the Treaty of Ghent in 1814 and the subsequent Rush-Bagot Agreement of 1817, it was permissible for the United States and Canada each to build and operate on the Great Lakes one six hundred ton armed ship. Canada never took advantage of this privilege, but in 1841 and 1842 the United States ordered plans drawn for the paddle-wheel, bark-rigged steamer *Michigan.* The hull was designed by Naval Constructor Samuel Hart, U.S.N., and the engines and boilers by C. W. Copeland. Both engines and boilers were built by Stackhouse & Tomlinson, then of Pittsburgh, Pennsylvania.

In 1843 the actual work of constructing the ship was started in Pittsburgh. The plates, frames and other iron parts were prepared there ready for assembling, and then were transported laboriously through the forest by oxen teams, overland to Erie, as the railroad was not yet available. At the foot of French Street in Erie, the work of assembling the ship was begun. The plates, of charcoal iron about three-eighths of an inch thick, were presumably beaten into shape with wooden mauls in a bed of sand. Three heavy box keelsons run the length of the ship, while two shorter keelsons form the foundation for the engine frame.

The *Michigan* was the first iron ship of the United States Navy and also the first iron ship to sail the waters of the Great Lakes. At present she is considered to be the oldest iron-hulled ship in the world. Even today the plates show little of the ravages of water, wind and weather, and it is stated that the ship never developed any structural weakness, despite the fact that she has experienced many a hard Great Lakes gale.

An iron ship in those days was a radically new departure, steam propulsion was hardly less so. Various crude forms of steam engines had been tried, and in the *Michigan* there was placed the very latest type of engine then developed. These were two inclined direct acting condensing engines, placed side by side, the cylinders being thirty-six inches in diameter with an eight foot stroke. Oddly enough these same engines still rest in the ship. They were used continuously during the eighty years that she sailed, and finally carried her to her home port at the end. With some repairs they could still be used. Her two original iron boilers lasted nearly fifty years, having been replaced during the winter of 1892 and 1893.

Wood served as fuel until coal become more readily available. In her early career the *Michigan* also carried sails as an aid to propulsion.

During 1843 the *Michigan* was launched into the waters of Erie Bay and was completed and outfitted the following year. An odd and interesting event is associated with her launching. Many curious spectators gathered at the ways to see the new iron ship take to the waters and doubt as to her ability to float was prevalent. As the vessel started down the ways to the water, she became stuck and could not be budged. The spectators eventually left the scene, and the story has it that, during the night, she launched herself, and was found floating proudly in the bay the next morning. Marine men state this feat is quite possible, due to the weight of the ship and consequent force of gravity.

The *Michigan* was placed in commission August 9, 1843, and made her first Great Lakes cruise in 1844 under the command of William P. Inman, who sailed her until October 24, 1845. Her command was then taken by Captain Stephen Champlin who, it is reported, was a cousin of Oliver Hazard Perry, and who commanded one of Perry's vessels, the *Scorpion*, in the battle of Lake Erie. Captain Champlin sailed the *Michigan* for three years, after which followed a list of thirty-seven commanders, the last being Lieutenant Commander William L. Morrison of Erie, Pennsylvania.

Among the outstanding details of the ship are: length, one hundred and sixty-eight feet; beam, twenty-seven feet; draft, ten feet; and displacement, six hundred tons.

Her wooden paddles are mounted on two twenty foot diameter wheels which are propelled by the engines previously described. The *Michigan* has carried various armament, replacing same as it was invented and improved. Her upper works have been changed since her launching, the cabins and deck houses being rebuilt to suit the work which she was doing at the time. As the ship stands today, the forward main deck is mostly clear. A large pilot house was built to serve the double purpose of navigating and chart preparing. A roomy bridge above was covered with awnings. Bridges extend over the paddle boxes amidships. The captain's cabin is aft on the main deck, true to the traditions of sailing ship days, and is today in fair condition. It consists of a roomy lounge with table, desk and library, two staterooms and bath, all paneled in rich dark woodwork. The aft part of the ship was known to her sailors as "the holy of holies" as only the highest ranking officers were permitted in these quarters. She carried one hundred and six men in her full crew.

Her career, in spite of her guns, has been peaceful. Only three outstanding events were particularly colorful. The first, just prior to the Civil War, was when she disbanded the Mormon colony which had settled on Beaver Island, in Lake Michigan, under the "rule" of "king" James Jesse Strang. Strang, a New York lawyer, caused great local difficulties between his band and the public authorities, who were unable to cope with him. Dissension broke out among his "subjects" and, to keep the peace, the *Michigan* was dispatched to the island "empire."

THE WOLVERINE

Her second event of importance was during the Civil War. Confederate refugees in Canada captured the passenger steamers *Philo Parsons* and *Island Queen* near Sandusky. They intended to overpower the crew of the *Michigan*, through a ruse, and turn her into a raider to prey upon lake shipping and ports; also to free the Confederate prisoners then held on Johnson's Island in Sandusky Bay. The daring plot failed, however, and resulted in the *Michigan* chasing the commandeered passenger boats into the open waters of Lake Erie, where they escaped.

Her third encounter was during the Fenian Invasion of Canada in 1866. The self-appointed and entirely unofficial raiders massed at Buffalo under the guise of laborers bound for the west. They numbered between one thousand and fifteen hundred. Capturing Canada was their ultimate objective.

With their green flag flying, they successfully crossed the Niagara River at Black Rock and took possession of the ruins of old Fort Erie on the Canadian shore. All this was accomplished without the knowledge of the United States authorities. The Fenian invaders were given arms as they came ashore at Fort Erie. These guns and ammunition had been previously hidden there by advance scouts.

The Canadians, upon learning of the sudden raiding party and the intended invasion, hurriedly mustered volunteers and engaged the unwelcome visitors. A desultory battle ensued in which the Fenians were eventually dispersed. They retreated in disorder to the river bank, seeking to return to Buffalo.

At this point the *Michigan* steamed to the scene and put the finishing touch to the untimely affair by taking the invaders as prisoners of the government.

It is also claimed for the *Michigan* that she was instrumental in giving to the medical world a living specimen of exposed human digestion. The ship was cruising among the Les Cheneaux Islands, when, at a port of call, a French Canadian woodman was brought to the ship for treatment by the ship's doctor. His abdomen had been accidentally chopped open, exposing the digestive operations to the surgeon's view.

The wounded man, Alexis St. Martin, was brought aboard the *Michigan* and taken to Mackinac Island where the phenomenon was studied and noted by Doctor William Beaumont, the army post surgeon stationed there. Doctor Beaumont is famous for his early and marvelous discoveries in intestinal surgery and gastric digestion. Several hospitals have been named in his memory, and his professional records have stood as medical authority for many years.*

It is said that the patient recovered to find a glass plate window in his abdomen, through which science continued its quest for knowledge; also that he survived Doctor Beaumont by almost twenty years. The island where the woodman was found was named for him, Saint Martin Island, and still carries this name.

The *Michigan* was used mostly in survey work and in training recruits in naval operations. Many of the modern Great Lakes charts are due to the work done aboard the old ship.

THE WOLVERINE

On June 21, 1905, her name was changed to *Wolverine*. This was caused by the naming of a new battleship on salt water, the *Michigan*. The old iron ship of the lakes then took the nickname of the state whose name she had previously carried.

During the Centennial celebration of Perry's victory in the Battle of Lake Erie, in the months of July, August and September of 1913, the *Wolverine* was in reflected glory. Throughout a cruise to Fairport, Cleveland, Sandusky, Put-in-Bay, Monroe, Toledo, Detroit, Green Bay, Milwaukee, Chicago and Buffalo she towed Perry's famous ship the *Niagara,* which had been raised and rebuilt. Hundreds of thousands viewed the two vessels in their parade of peace and goodwill up and down the Great Lakes. Giant celebrations were given the ships and crews at the ports of call and much interest was directed toward historical and nautical affairs of the Great Lakes country.

During the World War I the *Wolverine* again became active as a training ship and many a sailor recruit said goodbye to his city's sky line from the decks of this old ship.

But all careers must sometime end, and the old *Wolverine* was no exception. On August 12, 1923, while she was returning from a training cruise, steaming through the Straits of Mackinac, she had the misfortune to break a connecting rod on her port engine. Temporary repairs were at once made and it was found she could run under her own power at less than five miles per hour. So she continued on her run to Erie at this slow speed.

The fates were still against the old ship, as, during

that night, a strong summer gale blew up on Lake Huron, and the badly crippled *Wolverine* was forced to shelter at Harbor Beach, Michigan, until the next noon. After a slow and trying cruise, the grand old ship sailed triumphantly into Erie harbor, unassisted, and docked at the Public Pier. Her sailing days were over, as funds were not available to repair her damage and she lay floating idly at her dock for five years.

Her friends, however, watched her fondly and, with regret, noted how time was devastating what man had built. Realizing her probable fate would be to sink at her pier and be salvaged as junk, as a menace to the navigation she was built to protect, two old friends, one her last commander, William L. Morrison, and another Erie sailor, Captain P. J. Grant, took it upon themselves and arranged to have her towed to her present anchorage at Crystal Point in the famous Misery Bay. This was done with the aid of tugs on November 23, 1928. How the shades of her former commanders and crews must have cheered as these two conscientious sailors worked to protect the old ship! In her latest birth she is under the constant supervision of the Presque Isle State Park Commission, whose police watch over the veteran ship and see that she is protected from vandals.

However, even police cannot stop time from working its damage and, as a result, dry-rot has attacked decks and cabins, and the *Wolverine* now rests in a few feet of water, bravely appearing still to be riding the waves. Her broken connecting rod still hangs where it fell on that last eventful cruise. Her galley ranges, ice boxes and stores rooms are thick with dust. The white tile floor

56

in the once spotless galley is still trying to show through its covering of shore dirt, and her ports no longer house her once bristling guns.

So, for the present, ends the career of the *Wolverine,* the lakes' and navy's first iron ship, and the only United States Navy ship to ever carry arms on the Great Lakes; truly a monument to peace and goodwill on this frontier of two great neighboring nations.

It is hoped by all lovers of things marine, that, somehow, a way will be found to preserve this old and valuable relic of bygone days, and that, quite possibly, her future days might be turned to some less strenuous but useful occupation.

Note: As this book goes to press, it appears as though the *Wolverine* is doomed. Navy men have condemned the vessel and she will be sold for scrap unless something is done to change the present arrangements.

*Note: This tale of Alexis St. Martin was often told aboard the *Michigan* in her later days, but many of the details grew from sailors retelling. The correct version eliminates the *Michigan*. Alexis St. Martin was hit by the accidental discharge of a shotgun on Mackinac Island. He recovered to find a hole in his side through which Dr. William Beaumont, surgeon stationed at Fort Mackinac, could observe the man's digestive processes. This was the first time science had had such a satisfactory opportunity. Studies made by Dr. Beaumont on St. Martin's stomach have made medical history. The patient lived a strenuous life, fathered seventeen children, and died at eighty-three, twenty-seven years after the passing of Dr. Beaumont.

⚓ ⚓ ⚓ ⚓ ⚓ ⚓ ⚓ ⚓

CHAPTER SEVEN

EARLY PASSENGER SHIPS AND LATER ONES

The general public knows the passenger boats best. Only a comparatively few persons are acquainted with the prosaic freight boat. The Great Lakes passenger fleets have carried countless millions of people, from the early settlers heading for the new lands in the west, to the natty voyager of today.

The earliest travelers on the lakes were transported in sailing vessels primarily hauling freight but equipped in a crude fashion to accommodate a few passengers. In those days the men were housed separately from the women. Each occupied what was termed "Men's Cabin" and "Women's Cabin" respectively, and bunks were crudely built along the walls of the cabins to accommodate the overnight traveler. All quarters were in the hull, as the deck-house came later. Heat was furnished by a round stove, burning wood, placed in the center of the cabin. The food was poor and no regular schedules of sailing were attempted. The early settler was a hardy individual and knew nothing of luxuries. All this was before the railroads entered the field of transportation. The western bound pioneer arrived in Buffalo by stage and there looked for his transportation farther westward by the way of the Great Lakes.

As steam superseded sail, the passenger carrier on the

lakes came into its own. A thriving westward business was enjoyed by the early lake steamers. These vessels were built of wood and all used sails along with their steam power to economically speed up their travel. Wood from the nearby forests was the fuel burned in their boilers and, because storage capacity aboard was greatly limited, frequent stops for fuel had to be made.

The town of Black Rock, New York, located on the Niagara River, and now a part of the city of Buffalo, figured prominently in early shipping and shipbuilding on the lakes. It vied strongly with Buffalo until that city improved its harbor so that the early vessels could enter the port without having to anchor out in the lake and discharge cargo and passengers by lighters—a slow, dangerous and expensive operation. This lightering condition held true in many of the lake ports, notably Cleveland and Chicago. However, the embryo ports soon recognized the immense importance of a good harbor, and channels were made and docks constructed to enable ships to enter and leave with greater ease and safety.

The opening of the Erie Canal in 1825 from Albany, New York, on the Hudson River, to Buffalo, on Lake Erie, provided a great boom to shipping and passenger travel on the lakes. Westward migration proved less strenuous and much cheaper when done via the canal boats than by overland stage.

In 1830, five years after the completion of the Erie Canal, the Ohio Canal from Portsmouth, Ohio, on the Ohio River, to Cleveland, on Lake Erie, was opened to boat traffic. It offered the same travel advantages from southern Ohio to the lake country as was enjoyed by its eastern sister canal.

Over these inland waterways came hordes of pioneers, all bent on settling in the fertile lands around the Great Lakes. Commerce followed them, and soon the drowsy little terminals of Buffalo and Cleveland took on an activity that was destined to make great cities of them.

About the time the canals were opened, the steamboat on the lakes took on definite shape and it answered the need of the pioneer for more reliable transportation for himself, his goods and his produce. The earliest steamers were frail wooden crafts that could little stand the abuse that steam propulsion forced upon them, and they usually ended in a wreck along the shore. But, despite these difficulties, the shipbuilders persevered and shortly they were able to slide down their ways staunch steamers that could withstand all the abuses they were called upon to endure.

Then came the call for larger and better equipped passenger steamers. Travel became heavier, and bigger and faster ships were demanded. Better accommodations, and some of the luxuries of the trans-Atlantic, came with these new and larger ships. Thus it was that in the year 1844 the steamer *Empire State* was built at Cleveland and put into service on Lake Erie. She was two hundred and sixty feet in length, and all signs of sails had now vanished from her decks.

Several lake sailing ships attempted salt water voyages, notably the *Eureka*, of three hundred and fifty tons, which left Cleveland in 1849, bound for San Francisco, at the height of the California gold rush. She carried fifty-nine passengers and a full cargo of supplies. After a long voyage by way of the Saint Lawrence River, thence southward in the Atlantic Ocean along the eastern coasts of North and South America, around the treacherous Cape Horn, and thence northward in the Pacific Ocean along the western coasts of South America and North America, she finally came through the Golden Gate and dropped anchor in the harbor of San Francisco.

An outstanding voyage of a lake schooner started on July 19th, 1857, when the *Dean Richmond* cleared a Lake Michigan port for Europe. She arrived safely at Liverpool, England, on September 29th.

In 1854 the lakes saw the two thousand ton *Western World* built at Buffalo and enter the passenger service. She was the crowning glory of the shipbuilders' craft. The *Western World* was three hundred and forty-eight feet long, forty-five feet beam, with a deck width of seventy-two feet and draft of fourteen feet. Her hull was of white oak with decks of white pine. Her paddle wheels, thirty-nine feet in diameter, were as large as any then on the ocean. She ran between Buffalo, Cleveland and Detroit. Her interior, salon, dining rooms and cabins, were all embellished with the intricate hand-carved woodwork of the day, and carefully and expensively finished and decorated. She boasted of three hundred staterooms, and was a veritable floating palace and rightfully regarded as the finest ship on the lakes.

Other large passenger ships of those days were the *Northern Indiana* and the *Southern Michigan,* both around three hundred feet in length. There were also the *Plymouth Rock*, the *Mississippi*, the *Queen of the West*, the *Saint Lawrence*, the *Crescent City*, the *Western Metropolis* and an early *City of Buffalo*. All were of the side-wheel type with great arched trusses made of heavy timbers extending from the pilot house to the aft end of the ship.

The great *Western World*, however, was doomed to a very short active career. She sailed but three seasons and was then laid up by her owners. The same fate was meted out to the *Plymouth Rock*. The *Mississippi* and the *Queen of the West* were also subsequently removed from service. All these steamers were in good seaworthy condition, but it was found that they were being operated at a loss. They were all large and expensive to run.

In 1857 a financial panic swept lake shipping and was the direct cause of the removal of these good ships. The panic was brought about by competition of the railroads, which were stretching their iron rails throughout the length and breadth of the Great Lakes country. Travelers preferred the speedier rail to the slower water routes, and consequently disaster swept the costly operated lake steamers into the discard. The ship owners met the situation by building smaller vessels with less operating expense.

The giant *Western World*, the *Plymouth Rock*, the *Mississippi* and the *Queen of the West* were all tied up to a dock in Detroit, and all their splendor soon left them as they lay uncared for along the river front.

Six years later, in 1863, they were sold for dismantling

and towed to Buffalo, where the work was done. Their engines were all salvaged and placed into smaller new ships, then under construction. Their hulls were made into dry docks. It is said that the big hull of the *Western World* was towed to Bay City, Michigan, where it did such service for about fifteen years. The *Mississippi's* hull was taken to Cleveland where it also served for many years in the unromantic role of drydock. The *Plymouth Rock's* hull did similar duty at Buffalo.

Following the short and unfortunate existence of these early lake passenger giants, came an era of caution among the ship operators. Not wishing to be caught with any ship whose cost of operation proved excessive, they turned back to the smaller ship, with its consequent smaller operating costs. It was some forty years before such sized vessels as the *Western World* appeared again on the lakes. The intervening years showed a slow but steady increase in lake travel and in ship construction. The entering of coal into the field of steamer fuel proved of considerable assistance in operating the boats, inasmuch as longer voyages could be made without stopping to fuel. Eventually the cost of wood as boiler fuel became prohibitive as it became more and more scarce.

It is interesting to diverge for the moment and observe what the well dressed lake captain of the era of 1860 wore. We find him regaled in stately Prince Albert coat and high top plug hat. His heavy beard and sideburns gave him a ferocious appearance, which somehow seemed to please his vanity. At meal time he was to be found at the head of the ship's table, deftly carving the huge roast for the passengers. They had a language of their own, too, that proved puzzling to the inquiring landlubber passenger; with such phrases as, "Port side, aft, lady," or "Abaft the beam, mister."

Slowly confidence returned to the men who owned the lake steamers and they invested again in new ships, as they found that many travelers still preferred the more economical water transportation to that of the railroad. Definite sailing schedules and routes were adopted by the lines operating the passenger boats and a great deal of reliability was built into the business of lake transportation. Government interlake canals were opened and shallow channels were deepened. Most steamers had dropped the carrying of sails completely and depended entirely on their steam.

To the steamer *Vandalia,* built of wood, in 1840, goes the honor of being the first vessel to be propelled by a screw propeller in the stern of the ship. Its success was quickly proved and soon other steamers followed this type of propulsion. Today it is almost universally used on the ships of the Great Lakes. Only a few of the passenger steamers still have the side-wheel paddles.

Iron as a material for ships' hulls became a reality in 1843 with the building of the United States Navy Ship *Michigan* (later changed to *Wolverine*). The story of this very remarkable ship is told in another part of this book.

Three palatial combination passenger and freight steamers were built in 1871. They were the *India, China* and *Japan* for J. C. Evans and his son, E. T. Evans of Buffalo. This line of ships was operated for the Pennsylvania Railroad and known as the Anchor Line. The hulls of all three were of iron and were two hundred and ten feet keel length, thirty-two feet beam and fourteen feet draft.

These ships, accommodating one hundred and twenty passengers each, traveled the entire length of the Great Lakes from Buffalo to Duluth. These three sister steamers were reliable, seaworthy and very popular with the traveling public in the Gay Nineties. All were of the propeller type. All of the ships made a wonderful record for themselves in the thirty odd years that they operated. They were retired because of obsolescense. The three veteran ships then went to the shipyards and there were converted into freight carriers. Today, one of them, the *India,* now a barge, but still bearing her original name, is still active freighting steel between Lake Erie ports.

The *Japan* was eventually converted into the tanker *Roy K. Russell* and was active on Lake Ontario until she burned. The *China* became the *Westerian* and is said to have ended her career around the mouth of the Saint Lawrence River. The *India, China* and *Japan* were three illustrious old ships—monuments to their builders, their owners and to the men who sailed them.

To replace these retired veterans the Anchor Line ordered built the steamers *Tionesta,* in 1901, at Detroit; the *Juniata,* in 1904, at Cleveland; and lastly the *Octorara,* in 1910, at Wyandotte. Improvements that today are considered every-day necessities, such as electric lights, running water and call bells, were installed in these new five-decked ships.

65

LORE OF THE LAKES

The *Tionesta, Juniata* and *Octorara*, with a gross tonnage of four thousand three hundred and thirty tons each, were of the ocean type with a single propeller and a quadruple expansion reciprocating steam engine, which gave the boats an approximate speed of fifteen miles per hour.

With a length of three hundred and sixty-one feet, a beam of forty-five feet, and draft of seventeen feet, each of these white ships had a passenger capacity of five hundred and ninety-five, crew of one hundred and fifty-five, and dining room accommodations for two hundred and fifty persons.

These palatial steel vessels took their places on the run from Buffalo to Duluth as they came out and proved to be very popular with the public. The ships were named after three rivers in the State of Pennsylvania.

By an Interstate Commerce Commission ruling in 1916, separating rail and lake lines, the Anchor Line was dissolved and the three passenger ships, along with thirty freight boats, were taken over by The Great Lakes Transit Corporation of Buffalo.

Each summer sailing season would find these ships loaded with passengers enjoying themselves cruising the Great Lakes. They called at the larger ports from Buffalo to Duluth, giving service about every three days each way.

All went well with the ships, until the unfortunate burning of the liner *Morro Castle* in the Atlantic Ocean off Asbury Park, New Jersey, on September 8, 1934, in which one hundred and twenty-four lives were lost. This sea disaster caused the United States Bureau of Marine

EARLY PASSENGER SHIPS AND LATER ONES

Inspection and Navigation to greatly increase its requirements of safety aboard ships. A substantial sum of money would have been necessary to recondition the ships to meet these new requirements, and their owners decided that the work would not be done, at least not for the present, and the ships were consequently kept in port at Buffalo. It is claimed for these boats that never has there been an accident, a fire, or a life lost in the many years in which they have been operated.

So it was that the season of 1937 found the three boats idle. They are at present still at their docks awaiting their uncertain future. It is to be hoped that before long ways will be found to again send these ships on their pleasure cruises up and down the lakes, as in years gone by.

Two other palatial lake liners preceded the *Tionesta* in building and have long since passed out of service. They were the steamers *North West,* built in Cleveland in 1894, and the *North Land* in 1895. These twin ships are spoken of by people who have traveled on them as being the very last word in elegance and appointments, and would be so rated today if they were still in service. No expense was spared in the building and operating of the ships. They were built for The Northern Steamship Company, which was owned principally by the late James J. Hill, famous as the railroad empire builder of his day. At that time he was the builder and owner of the Great Northern Railroad which stretched from Duluth to the West Coast. Mr. Hill was also heavily interested in other railroads which ran from Buffalo to the East Coast. He needed a connecting link for the two rail systems. Thus it was that he organized the Northern Steamship Company and ordered the palatial steamers *North West* and *North Land* constructed. A traveler could then ride from coast to coast across the continent on Hill controlled lines.

Pomp and grandeur prevailed aboard these ships. Hill determined to have the finest of everything aboard his lake fleet. Into it was built all that could be found in the most modern salt water liners of that day. Every detail was for completeness. It is said that a certain chef in the east was famous for his onion soup. Hill arranged for him to be aboard his fleet, where his onion soup was soon renowned from Buffalo to Duluth. The most reputable men on the lakes were hired to make up crews of both ships. Many of them were sent aboard ocean liners to study their methods before they were sent to the *North West* or *North Land*. President McKinley, then governor of Ohio, was a guest aboard the *North West* on her trial trip, as were many other dignitaries and industrial captains of the day. Marine men, the lakes over, marveled as they watched the swift ships cut the clear lake waters.

The *North West* and *North Land* measured three hundred and eighty-six feet from stem to stern, with forty-four feet beam, twenty-six feet depth and five thousand gross tonnage. The hulls were painted white and they carried three smoke stacks which were yellow with a black band around the top, the center stack having a large white star mounted on it which was illuminated at night. Each consumed eight tons of coal an hour when cruising at full speed. Passenger quarters were all finished in white mahogany and walnut. It is reported that these great ships were not a financial success in spite of the fact that their passenger lists were filled every trip. The *North West* ran from Buffalo to Duluth, while the *North Land* operated from Chicago to Buffalo. They started their season in early June and finished in late September.

On June 3rd, 1911, while the two ships lay at their docks in Buffalo being fitted out for the coming season, a devastating fire swept the interior of the *North West*. She sank at her pier during the fire, and damage, said to amount to almost a quarter of a million dollars, was done to the ship. It spelled the end of the *North West* as a luxury lake liner. She was raised and left at her dock until 1918. The *North Land* was not damaged and she sailed on schedule.

The World War caused a serious shortage of ships on the high seas and scouts were sent over the world ports in search of suitable vessels for war service. The *North West* was in order for such work. It is said that during this period she was sold five times. Eventually her engines and boilers were taken out and shipped to the coast for installation in salt water ships.

The hull of the *North West,* too long to pass through the locks of the Saint Lawrence River to tidewater, was stripped of all that made it a passenger ship. It was then cut in two, athwartships, at Buffalo, to enable each half to be floated separately through the locks and thus towed to the Atlantic seaboard. It was intended that once the two parts of the hull reached tidewater they would be placed together again to form a sound hull for ocean travel.

This, however, was not to be. As the forward section was being towed across Lake Ontario on November 28, 1918, it was engulfed in a sudden lake squall. The unwieldy half of a ship sank beneath the waves. Ten men aboard were saved, one of whom later died of exposure.

The after section of the *North West* had better fortune. It navigated successfully the waters between Buffalo and Levis, Quebec. There a new forward section, to replace the one lost, was made and fitted to it. It was given a new name, *Maplecourt*. Gone were the days when happy throngs went over her gangplank, and smartly dressed couples danced lightly in her brilliant ball room. Now she was just a lowly freight boat.

But the *Maplecourt* was destined to again see the Great Lakes. In August of 1921, she became one of the great fleet of the Canada Steamship Company, the largest fleet on the lakes, and was again cut in two and towed back to Buffalo, where she was reassembled and started transporting coal and grain up and down the lakes.

Fate still pursued the ship. Late in the fall of 1929, she was wrecked at the northern end of Lake Huron, near Drummond Island. Winter closed in on the wrecked ship and she was locked fast in the ice until navigation opened the following spring. Then she was repaired and refloated and was taken over by the Sin-Mac Lines and converted into a wrecking and salvaging ship. Since that time the interesting old ship has figured in rescue work of many distressed vessels. At present she is at her home port, Sarnia, Ontario, awaiting the call of a boat in trouble.

The sister ship, *North Land,* did not share the glamour of the *North West.* The *North Land* in 1919 was sold and also cut in two at Buffalo and towed to Quebec. This was the last the lakes saw of the fine ship. Her new owners intended to put her in the third class travel trade between Canada and Italy. This, however, never materialized, as the owners changed their plans. The *North Land* laid at the dock until 1921 when she was dismantled and reduced to scrap.

Such is the interesting tale of the *North West* and her sister ship, the *North Land.* Old-timers along the Saint Clair River recall the impressive sight of the great white ships as they plowed their way up the river toward Lake Huron at nightfall, with their brilliant lights sparkling across the darkening waters, and their white hulls dimly outlined in the fast approaching darkness. A fitting picture by which to remember the "Queens of the Inland Seas."

Many fine old passenger ships ran out of Detroit, and some of the lakes' finest still do. In former days the great passenger lines sailing out of Detroit were owned largely by wealthy local families, the Dustins, Campbells, Bielmans and McMillans, and it was the eager desire of the management of these lines to possess the largest and finest boats that money could procure. The building programs of these lines were the pride and boast of the Great Lakes for many years.

71

One outstanding fleet that has disappeared completely from the lakes is that of the old White Star Line of Detroit. This line was probably at its peak about 1910. Its trim fleet of five spotless white ships was an inspiring sight as passengers would crowd aboard the boats for a gala holiday on the water, as the ships were docked in the Detroit River. The fleet then consisted of the flagship, *Tashmoo*, the *City of Toledo*, the *Greyhound*, the *Owana* and the *Wauketa*. The line encountered difficulties later and today these fine ships are gone and all but forgotten. The *Tashmoo* and the *City of Toledo* ran between Detroit and Port Huron. The *Greyhound* and the *Owana* ran between Detroit and Toledo. The *Wauketa* was a special excursion ship.

The Ashley and Dustin Line is an old established Detroit concern that has successfully operated passenger ships out of that port for many years. The line has operated such famous ships as the *Dart*, the *Alaska*, the *Frank E. Kirby*, the *Put-In-Bay*, and others, on the run between Detroit, Put-In-Bay and Sandusky.

The steamer *Alaska* was the fast boat of her period, 1875 to 1890. She was a side-wheeler with a walking beam engine. She ran eight months each season out of Detroit, serving the Lake Erie Islands and Sandusky, carrying fish in the spring, excursions to Put-In-Bay during the summer, and grape and peach crops in the fall, usually laying up about Thanksgiving time.

The *Alaska* was dismantled in 1890. The engine was installed in a new steel hull equipped with all the modern devices of the day, finer hull lines, Monitor boilers, forced draft, trim tanks, electric lights and feathering buckets. The new ship was designed by and named for the great marine architect, Frank E. Kirby, who designed so many of the later sidewheel passenger steamers on the Great Lakes, numerous lake freighters and many ships for foreign trade.

The *Frank E. Kirby* was a success from the start, and was remarkable for her speed. She put up a record of two hours and fifty-four minutes for the sixty mile run to Put-In-Bay from Detroit. This record has never been equaled, and likely never will be as, in the old days, the steamers could speed in the Detroit River, while now they must check down owing to channel regulations.

All the fast steamers would take after the steamer *Frank E. Kirby*, and her captain, Arthur J. Fox, flaunted them all by carrying a broom at the masthead, which, in symbol, swept away all contestants. The fast passenger steamers *City of Alpena* and *City of Mackinac* had many a hot brush with the *Frank E. Kirby*. The steamer *Greyhound* was fast, but Captain Fox always came out ahead. The *Idlewild, Columbia, Arrow* and *City of Toledo* tried their best to outrun the *Kirby*, but the "Flyer of the Lakes" showed her stern to all of them. The fast *Tashmoo* and the *Frank E. Kirby* never met in a speed contest.

The steamer *City of Erie* on her trial trip pursued the *Kirby* from Detroit all the way to Put-In-Bay, endeavoring to overtake her. In spite of the fact that the engines of the *City of Erie* were new and powerful, she was not able to catch up with the heavily laden *Kirby*.

All the old-timers around the lakes remember the famous race between the steamers *Tashmoo* and *City of Erie* on Lake Erie (which is described in detail in another chapter in this book). The *Frank E. Kirby* made a special excursion on that occasion and ran along with the racing steamers, allowing them a wide berth. It is reported by the *Kirby's* crew that she kept up well with the racers. The *Kirby's* passengers enjoyed a thrilling spectacle.

In 1911 the owners of the *Kirby* brought out the new steamer *Put-In-Bay* which eventually replaced the *Kirby*. However, the latter vessel remained on the route until 1920, when she was sold.

During July, 1938, the Detroit and Windsor ferry line discontinued operation, laying up the large ferries *Cadillac* and *LaSalle*. International commuters had used this ferry service for seventy-five years previous. A new bridge and a vehicular tunnel under the river were competitive factors in the closing of the ferry line. A ferry service is still in operation between Detroit and Walkerville, Ontario.

The steamer *Arrow,* which plied the run from Sandusky to the Lake Erie Islands burned severely while at her dock in Put-In-Bay in the fall of 1922. She was replaced by the sidewheel steamer *Chippewa*. The *Chippewa* started service as the United States Revenue Cutter *William A. Fessendon* in 1884. Rebuilt in 1909 as a passenger vessel, she was re-named the *Chippewa,* and entered service in the waters around Mackinac Island and the Soo.

In 1923 her home port was changed to Sandusky, Ohio,

where she took over the run of the burned *Arrow*. The *Chippewa* is two hundred and twelve feet long, with one hundred and ninety-eight feet keel, twenty-eight feet hull beam, and fifty-four feet beam overall. She is of steel construction, four hundred and fifty-two gross tons, built in Buffalo, has ten staterooms and can carry seven hundred day passengers. She is at present in Sandusky.

During the season of 1939 the *Chippewa* did not operate, as her owners brought the steamer *City of Hancock* from Lake Superior and put it on the run formerly covered by the *Chippewa*.

In the harbor of Cleveland in 1939 could be seen several old lake passenger liners either dismantled or out of commission. The stripped hull of the *City of Buffalo* (the burning of which is told in detail elsewhere in this book) lay awaiting its dubious future. Nearby was the day excursion boat, *Goodtime,* which operated last in 1938 on the Cleveland, Cedar Point and Put-in-Bay run.

This steamer, formerly the *City of Detroit II,* a D & C liner, is a sidewheeler, built in 1890, and rebuilt into a day boat for the C & B Line in 1924. The *Goodtime* therefore has the excellent record of nearly fifty years of passenger service on the Great Lakes.

Preceding the *Goodtime* on the Cleveland to Put-in-Bay run was the little sidewheeler *State of Ohio*. This historic old passenger boat figured prominently in the early days of the Detroit and Cleveland Navigation Company, and later in those of the Cleveland and Buffalo Transit Company. The *State of Ohio* burned to a total wreck at her dock at East Ninth Street in Cleveland on May 20,

1924, while workmen were preparing her for the season. Her hull was afterwards salvaged and used as a sand barge.

At another dock on the lake front in Cleveland in 1939 lay the steamer *City of Erie,* another veteran with forty odd years of faithful service to her credit. She sailed last in 1938 on the Cleveland and Buffalo run for the C & B Line. Whether either the *Goodtime* or the *City of Erie* ever will operate again depends on the travel demands on the lakes and the possibility of refitting these ships to meet such demands.

The number of passenger ships sailing out of the port of Chicago has of recent years been greatly reduced. The Goodrich Transit Company, established by Captain A. E. Goodrich in 1856, with one small wood-burning steamer, the *Huron,* running from Chicago to Milwaukee, flourished for over eighty years. Ever careful to improve its lake passenger and freight service on Lake Michigan, the company acquired many ships in the years that it operated. The Goodrich Line, like many other similar lake lines, was not able to withstand the overwhelming competition of the automobile, the truck, the airplane, and other fast transportation mediums, and consequently left the field.

During the year 1930 the Goodrich Line had a very fine fleet of passenger ships, all of them of the propeller type, the most famous being its *Christopher Columbus.* This big ship was the only whaleback type passenger ship ever built and therefore created a great amount of attention from strangers and marine men alike. Built in Duluth in 1892 by Alexander McDougall, she was sent to Chicago and put to work the following year carrying passengers to the World's Fair.

Her trip was six miles from the downtown docks at Randolph Street to Jackson Park, and it is estimated that, in that year, she carried approximately two million passengers without the loss of a single life. It is said that she could discharge her load of five thousand passengers in five minutes. She was later put on the Chicago to Milwaukee day run, on which she served many years. She was three hundred and sixty-two feet long, forty-two feet beam, and fifteen hundred gross tons. Five steel turrets projected from her promenade deck up through the hurricane deck, similar to a battleship. With her five thousand horse-power engines and eighteen foot propeller, she could travel at the fast speed of eighteen miles per hour, often carrying four thousand passengers on a trip. She went out of business several years ago and was dismantled at Manitowoc, Wisconsin, in 1936. It is said that the *Christopher Columbus* carried more passengers during her career than any other lake steamer.

Other ships of the Goodrich fleet in 1930 were the *City of Grand Rapids, Alabama, Carolina, City of Saugatuck, City of St. Joseph, City of Benton Harbor, City of Holland, Bainbridge* and the *Theodore Roosevelt.*

The *City of Saugatuck* and the *City of St. Joseph* are now barges operating on the New York State Barge Canal. They are two hundred and sixty-six feet keel and thirty-eight feet beam. The *Virginia,* an earlier Goodrich boat, left the Great Lakes and is now reported as sailing between Los Angeles and Catalina Island in the Pacific. Another early Goodrich boat, the *Missouri,* was recently seriously damaged by fire as she lay idle at a Wisconsin port. The *Alabama* was taken over by another owner and is at present operating from Lake Erie to Duluth in the passenger trade.

At least one passenger fleet of lake boats can boast of a Fifty-Year Club. It is the Detroit and Cleveland Navigation Company in Detroit. The Fifty-Year Club is composed of employees who have been with the line for fifty or more years. These men have actually outlived the early ships of their fleet. For over seventy years the ships of this fleet have served the lake traveler.

The original Detroit and Cleveland fleet began operations about 1850 with two wooden steamers, the *Southerner* and the *Baltimore.* Then followed many old-timers such as: *Forest City, Saint Louis, Samuel Ward, May Queen, Morning Star, R. N. Rice,* an early *North West,* and *Saginaw.* In 1878 the first *City of Detroit* was launched. This was a composite hull ship. In 1883 the first iron steamer of the line, the *City of Mackinac,* was constructed. Early records show several steamers at various times carried the names *City of Detroit* and *City of Cleveland.*

EARLY PASSENGER SHIPS AND LATER ONES

Today upon the walls of the company's waiting rooms in Detroit are some very interesting hull models of their fleet. At a glance one can see the vast improvements that have been made in the ships, particularly in the size of hulls, starting with the little steamer *State of New York* and in succession: the *State of Ohio, City of the Straits, City of St. Ignace, City of Alpena, City of Mackinac*. All of these ships have long since passed into oblivion as passenger ships. Then comes the *City of Detroit II*, which left the D & C fleet years ago. The present fleet takes the attention at this point with the steamers *Eastern States, Western States, City of Cleveland III, City of Detroit III*, and ending with the flagships, *Greater Buffalo* and *Greater Detroit*.

What the early passenger ships and later ones have done to establish the large cities that now thrive on the shores of the Great Lakes, can never be measured. Many a settler obtained his first view of his to-be-adopted city from the deck of one of these vessels. The boats held cherished memories for these people and for the business men of the lake marine.

The business of transportation moves quickly forward and perhaps the grand old ships of the lakes are too slow for some modern hurried travelers, but they served well the travelers and shippers of yesterday. To these folks, to the men who manned the ships, and to the lovers of lake romance, the old ships will always hold a deep and hearty interest.

The passenger fleet on the lakes in 1938 had dwindled to a total of but one hundred and forty-one vessels, large and small, pleasure craft and ferries, including United States and Canadian registry; car ferries not included. A great many of these one hundred and forty-one ships are not in operation, being tied fast to their docks, and it appears likely that they may never again be used to haul passengers. Some are obsolete, some in bad state of repair, some insolvent, and many others for various reasons are not being operated.

Gone from the lakes are most of the steamers mentioned in this chapter. That there will be a record of these ships kept for the future; that the record will be interesting; and that the ships be not entirely forgotten, are the paramount thoughts in offering this chapter.

NOTE—As this book goes to press several changes have occurred in the status of some of the vessels mentioned.

The *Maplecourt*, one-half of which was the old *North West*, is leaving the Great Lakes once more to engage in war time service on the high seas. She is again to be cut in two, hauled thus to tidewater, and re-assembled. Will the historic old steamer ever return to the lakes?

The *Tionesta, Juniata* and *Octorara* are reported as having been sold to new owners. Rumors are that the lake triplets will be used on the oceans as troop ships or that they may be reduced to scrap.

The *Chippewa* is being dismantled at Sandusky, Ohio.

The *Goodtime* was taken to Erie, Pennsylvania, to be dismantled.

PICTORIAL
SECTION

CHAPTER EIGHT

HAPPY ECHOES

THE STORY OF THE LAKES
TOLD IN PICTURES

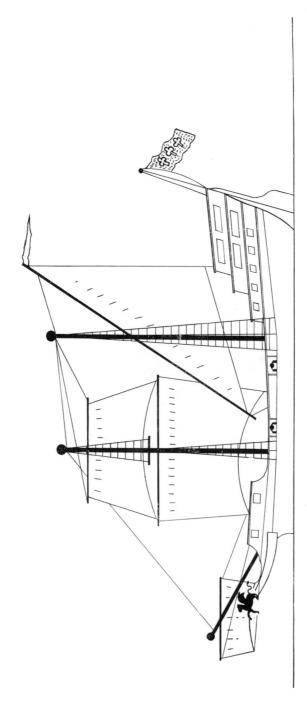

The Griffin, Built by La Salle in 1679, Disappeared About Four Months After Her Launching, The First Accredited Vessel of the White Man to Sail the Great Lakes.

PERRY TRANSFERS HIS FLAG TO THE *Niagara* IN THE BATTLE OF LAKE ERIE, SEPT. 10, 1813.
From a painting in the Capitol, Washington, by W. H. Powell

"The Rebuilt *Niagara* (In Cleveland in 1913) Looked Exactly as She Did . . . One Hundred Years Previous." U. S. S. *Wolverine* at Same Dock in Background

"Lack of Funds (in 1939 at Erie, Pa.) Halted Work of Restoration . . . The Partially Rebuilt *Niagara* Stands on the Ways."

Schooner *Henry C. Richards*, A Benham Windjammer
From a Pastel

LORE OF THE LAKES

A GREAT LAKES' SCHOONER
OF BY-GONE DAYS

W. S. Foster Photo

OLD STATE LOCK AT THE SOO. BUILT IN 1855.

Young Photo

SCHOONER *Our Son.* LAST OF THE LAKES' WINDJAMMERS. NAMED IN MEMORY OF FIRST OWNER'S SON WHO WAS DROWNED SHORTLY BEFORE HER LAUNCHING AT LORAIN ABOUT 1872. FOUNDERED OFF SHEBOYGAN, WIS., SEPT. 26, 1930, WITH CARGO OF PULP WOOD, CREW OF SEVEN RESCUED BY STEAMER *William Nelson.*   Capt W. J. Taylor Photo

SCHOONER C. K. *Clint;* O. B. SMITH, MASTER, ENTERING
ESCANABA HARBOR WITH COAL, AUGUST 21, 1890.

Detroit Harbor in 1836. From a Painting by William James Bennett Owned by the Detroit Institute of Arts.

One of the Last Windjammers on the Lakes, Passing St. Clair, Mich., in 1910. Schooner *Hattie Hutt*, Formerly *F. B. Stockbridge*, Built in 1873 at Saugatuck, Mich.

First Steamboat on Upper Great Lakes; *Walk-in-the-Water*, 1818 to 1821.
Courtesy Great Lakes News.

Young Photo

EARLY SOO LOCK FROM A DRAWING

DRAWING SHOWING EARLY SIDEWHEEL PASSENGER STEAMER *E. Ward* OF THE LAKE SUPERIOR LINE LEAVING THE SOO LOCKS.   Young Photo

"In Her Early Career the *Michigan* (Now *Wolverine*) . . .
Carried Sails as an aid to Propulsion."

U. S. S. Wolverine IN 1939—BOW VIEW

U. S. S. Wolverine IN 1939—STERN VIEW

THE *Vandalia*—FIRST PROPELLER ON THE LAKES

Courtesy Great Lakes News

TUG *Samson* AND TOW, PASSING FORT GRATIOT LIGHT, ABOUT 1880. SCHOONERS IN TOW—H. C. *Richards, Queen City, Z. Chandler, C. H. Johnson* AND *Reindeer.*

From a Painting by R. D. Wilcox

EARLY STEAMER *Harlem* OF NEW YORK CENTRAL & HUDSON RIVER R. R. LINE.
NOTE THE SAILS AND TWO STACKS.

Courtesy Great Lakes News

CIVIL WAR DAYS LAKE PASSENGER STEAMER ON LAKE ERIE
ISLANDS—SANDUSKY RUN.

EARLY IRON FREIGHTER, *Onoko*—1882 TO 1915. "TRUE
PROTOTYPE OF THE MODERN FREIGHTER."

Wooden Lumber Hooker C. F. Curtis, "Sailed Away" on Lake Superior With Two Barges, in 1914.

Young Photo

Lake Passenger Steamer of the Gay Nineties. Three Such Ships Sailed the Lakes; *Japan*, Shown Above; *China* and *India*. Young Photo

India, Converted Into a Barge, as she is Today. She was a Sister Ship of the *Japan*, Shown on Opposite Page.

Wooden Freighter *Orinoco* With a Two Barge Tow

Young Photo

"Lumber Hooker . . . Lost on Lake Erie in the 'Black Friday' Storm"
Young Photo

WOODEN STEAMER *City of Glasgow*

BARGE *Abyssinia*. BOTH EARLY HUTCHINSON LINE BOATS

Passenger Steamer *Christopher Columbus* — 1892 to 1936. Is Said to Have Carried More Passengers During Her Career Than Any Other Ship Afloat.
Ross & Wiley Photo

WOODEN FREIGHTER *Yakima*—FIRST SHIP ON THE LAKES TO
CARRY ELECTRIC LIGHTS.   Young Photo

STEEL FREIGHTER *Superior City*, 1898 to 1920. "SERVED HER
PURPOSE AS A STEPPING-STONE TO BETTER VESSELS."
Young Photo

STEAMER *North West*—BYGONE PALATIAL PASSENGER SHIP—AT THE SOO
Young Photo

ANOTHER VIEW OF THE *North West*
Courtesy Great Lakes News

PASSENGER STEAMER *Eastland* IN HER HEYDAY
ON JULY 25, 1915, SHE ROLLED OVER AT CHICAGO, THEREBY CAUSING THE
WORST SINGLE DISASTER EVER TO OCCUR ON THE GREAT LAKES. 835 PERSONS
LOST THEIR LIVES.

Ross & Wiley Photo

U. S. S. *Wilmette* AT PRESENT—FORMERLY THE PASSENGER STEAMER *Eastland*
Ross & Wiley Photo

STEAMER *Eastland* ON LAKE ERIE

Bishop Photo

OPENING DAY CELEBRATION, 1914, AT THE DAVIS, OR THIRD
LOCK, AT THE SOO. STEAMER *A. C. Dinkey*, AT RIGHT.

Young Photo

STEAMER *Bannockburn*—THE MYSTERIOUS "FLYING DUTCHMAN" OF LAKE SUPERIOR. ONLY AN OAR WAS EVER FOUND, EIGHTEEN MONTHS AFTER SHE DISAPPEARED.

Young Photo

WHALEBACK STEAMER *James B. Colgate*, LOST ON LAKE ERIE IN "BLACK FRIDAY" STORM.

Young Photo

WOODEN SHIPBUILDING AT MONK'S SHIPYARD, SANDUSKY.
STEAMER *A. Wehrle, Jr.,* ON THE WAYS. WHEN WORKMEN
WORE DERBY HATS WHILE THEY LABORED.

Bishop Photo

SANDUSKY DOCKS ABOUT 1885 TO 1890. STEAMERS *Arrow*, *A. Wehrle, Jr.*, AND *R. B. Hayes*.

Bishop Photo

LORE OF THE LAKES

A LAKE ERIE PLEASURE BOAT IN THE 90's

Bishop Photo

STEAMER *Arrow* RAN BETWEEN SANDUSKY AND LAKE ERIE
ISLANDS. BURNED AT HER DOCK IN 1922.

Bishop Photo

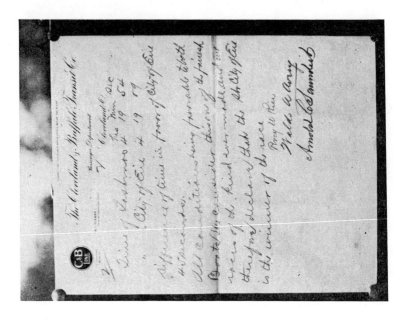

FACSIMILE OF OFFICIAL JUDGE'S LETTER ANNOUNCING OUTCOME OF THE FAMOUS RACE

Courtesy C. B. Percy, Detroit

Monson Photo

DETROIT WATERFRONT ABOUT 1910. STEAMER *Tashmoo* IN MID-STREAM.

PASSENGER STEAMER *City of Erie* IN CLEVELAND IN 1939.

STEAMER *Frank E. Kirby* RAN BETWEEN DETROIT AND
SANDUSKY, 1890 TO 1920.

THE END FOR THE *I. Watson Stephenson*—ABOUT TO BE SUNK
OFF CLEVELAND IN 1935 AFTER 40 YEARS OF SERVICE.

POPULAR LAKE LINER *Tionesta.* TWO OTHER SHIPS, *Juniata* AND *Octorara* WERE EXACT DUPLICATES. SAILED THE GREAT LAKES FROM EARLY 1900's UNTIL 1936.
Young Photo

EARLY WINTER—THE LAST TRIP DOWN

Young Photo

HELD FAST IN THE ICE AT THE SOO IN DECEMBER

Young Photo

THANKSGIVING DAY

Young Photo

APRIL NAVIGATION ON THE LAKES

Young Photo

The vessels shown on pages 122, 123, 124, 125, 126 and 127 were all lost or wrecked in the Big Storm of 1913. The story is told in Chapter Thirteen of this book.

CANADIAN FREIGHTER *James Carruthers* LOST ON LAKE HURON

BULK FREIGHTER *Hydrus*, SANK IN LAKE HURON

CANADIAN FREIGHTER *Leafield*, SANK IN LAKE SUPERIOR

BULK FREIGHTER *John A. McGean,* LOST IN LAKE HURON

PACKAGE FREIGHTER *Regina,* SANK IN LAKE HURON

COMPOSITE PHOTO OF STEAMER *Charles S. Price*
UPPER HALF SHOWS THE VESSEL BEFORE THE
BIG STORM. LOWER HALF AS SHE APPEARED IN
LAKE HURON FOR A FEW DAYS AFTER THE BIG
STORM. SHE EVENTUALLY SANK.

Young Photo

FREIGHTER *Isaac M. Scott*, LOST IN LAKE HURON

FREIGHTER *L. C. Waldo*, WRECKED ON LAKE SUPERIOR

CANADIAN FREIGHTER *Wexford*, SANK IN LAKE HURON

FREIGHTER *Argus*, SANK IN LAKE HURON

CANADIAN STEAMER *Kamloops* DISAPPEARED ON LAKE SUPERIOR IN 1927
Young Photo

Steamer *Wm. H. Wolf*, Upbound in Soo Locks With a Deck Load of Automobiles.

Wrecking Whaleback *J. T. Reid* (Formerly *Washburn*) at Cleveland About 1936.

FREIGHTER *Wm. A. Paine* LEAVING SOO LOCK, DOWN-BOUND

FREIGHTERS LOCKING UP AT SOO LOCKS

STEAMER *City of Buffalo* AFTER THE FIRE

STEAMER *City of Buffalo* LATER STRIPPED TO MAIN DECK

BEAUTIFUL PERRY MONUMENT AT PUT-IN-BAY, OHIO
STEAMER *Chippewa* PASSING

STEAMERS *James A. Farrell* AND *Seeandbee* AT THE SOO

STEAMER *Charles L. Hutchinson*—TYPICAL MODERN LAKE BULK
FREIGHTER.

Air View of the Four Soo Locks on Which "The Government Spent . . . A Total of About 27 Million Dollars." Soo Rapids in Center. Canadian Lock in Background.

Excursion Steamer Between Detroit, Put-in-Bay and Sandusky

BIG PASSENGER STEAMER *Seeandbee* AT A SOO DOCK

STEAMER *Seeandbee* AT MACKINAC ISLAND

BOW VIEW OF OVERNIGHT STEAMER *City of Detroit III*
OPERATING BETWEEN CLEVELAND AND DETROIT

PLEASURE CRUISE SHIP *South American*

LORE OF THE LAKES

CANADIAN PASSENGER CRUISE STEAMER *Noronic*

PASSENGER CRUISE STEAMER *Alabama*

STEAMER *Greater Buffalo*. TOGETHER WITH HER TWIN SHIP *Greater Detroit*
THEY MAINTAIN NIGHTLY SERVICE BETWEEN DETROIT AND BUFFALO. LARGEST
PASSENGER SHIPS ON THE GREAT LAKES.

OVERNIGHT PASSENGER BOAT *City of Cleveland III* OPERATING BETWEEN
CLEVELAND AND DETROIT

CARFERRY *Windsor* AT DETROIT

CANAL MOTOR-SHIP *Clevelander*

LARGEST FREIGHTER ON THE GREAT LAKES—A SELF-UNLOADER
Young Photo

ONE OF THE NEWEST BULK FREIGHTERS ON THE LAKES
Young Photo

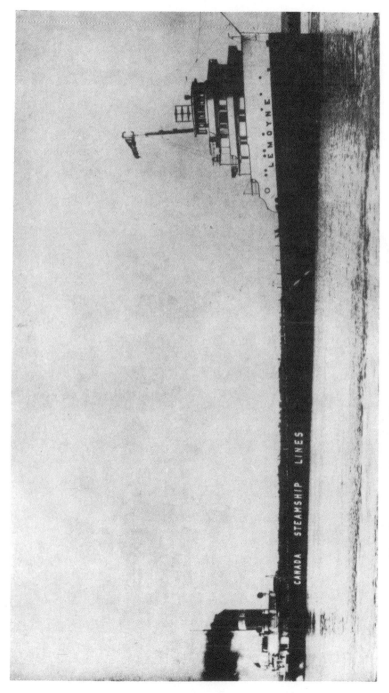

THE *Lemoyne*—LARGEST CANADIAN BULK FREIGHTER ON THE GREAT LAKES
Young Photo

FREIGHTER *Harry Coulby*—Broke Her Own Record for Largest Ore Cargo Carried.

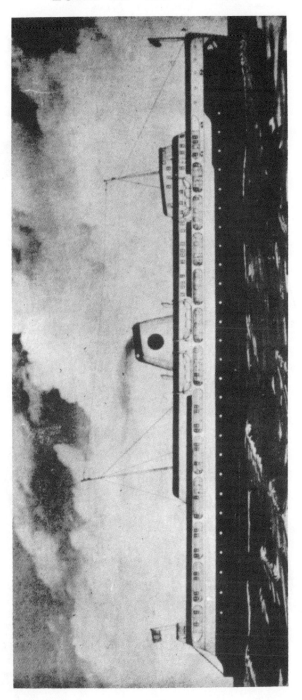

Drawing of New Streamlined Carferry *City of Midland* Launched at Manitowoc, Wis., Late in 1940. Will Operate Across Lake Michigan

CHAPTER NINE

VESSEL STACKS OF PROMINENT GREAT LAKES FLEETS

BETHLEHEM FLEET

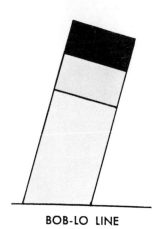

BOB-LO LINE

BOLAND & CORNELIUS
FLEET

BRADLEY
TRANSPORTATION CO.

BROWN STEAMSHIP CO.

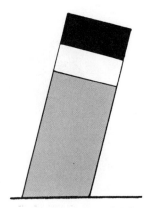

CANADA STEAMSHIP
LINES, Ltd.

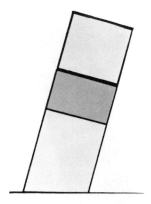

CHICAGO, DULUTH &
GEORGIAN BAY LINE

CLEVELAND & BUFFALO
TRANSIT COMPANY

CLEVELAND CLIFFS
FLEET

COLUMBIA
TRANSPORTATION CO.

FORD MOTOR CO.

FRANKLIN STEAMSHIP
COMPANY

GARTLAND STEAMSHIP
FLEET

GREAT LAKES STEAMSHIP
COMPANY

GREAT LAKES TOWING CO.

GREAT LAKES TRANSIT
CORPN.

HANNA FLEET

HURON TRANSPORTATION
COMPANY

HUTCHINSON FLEET

IMPERIAL OIL SHIPPING
CO., Ltd.

INLAND FLEET

INTERLAKE STEAMSHIP
FLEET

PICKANDS-MATHER & CO.,
MGRS.

JONES & LAUGHLIN, INTER-
STATE STEAMSHIP
COMPANY

KELLEY ISLAND LIME &
TRANSPORT COMPANY

KINSMAN TRANSIT FLEET

MIDLAND STEAMSHIP
LINE, Inc.

MINNESOTA-ATLANTIC
TRANSIT COMPANY

NICHOLSON TRANSIT FLEET

PATERSON STEAMSHIPS, Ltd.

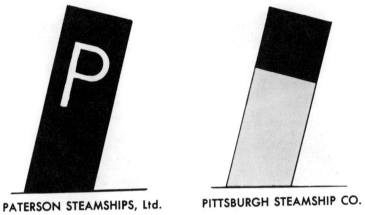

PITTSBURGH STEAMSHIP CO.

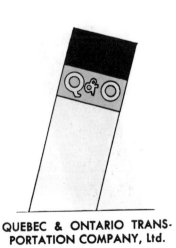

QUEBEC & ONTARIO TRANS-
PORTATION COMPANY, Ltd.

REISS STEAMSHIP FLEET

SARNIA STEAMSHIPS, Ltd.

STANDARD OIL CO.,
OF INDIANA

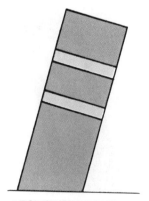

TOMLINSON FLEET

TREE LINE NAVIGATION
CO., Ltd.

U. S. STEEL PRODUCTS
COMPANY

VALLEY CAMP FLEET

WILSON TRANSIT COMPANY

WYANDOTTE TRANSPORTA-
TION COMPANY

U. S. DEPARTMENT OF COMMERCE,
WEATHER BUREAU SIGNALS

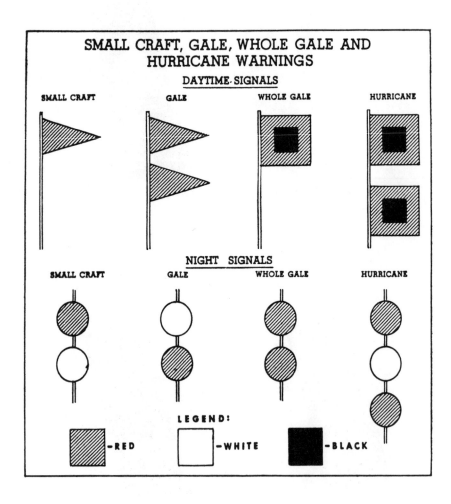

LORE OF THE LAKES

U. S. DEPARTMENT OF COMMERCE, WEATHER BUREAU

SMALL CRAFT, GALE, WHOLE GALE AND HURRICANE WARNINGS

EXPLANATION OF DISPLAY SIGNALS

SMALL CRAFT WARNING: One red pennant displayed by day and a red light over a white light at night to indicate winds up to 38 miles an hour (33 knots) and/or sea conditions dangerous to small craft operations are forecast for the area.

GALE WARNING: Two red pennants displayed by day and a white light above a red light at night to indicate winds ranging from 39 to 54 miles an hour (34 to 48 knots) are forecast for the area.

WHOLE GALE WARNING: A single square red flag with a black center displayed during daytime and two red lights at night to indicate winds ranging from 55 to 73 miles an hour (48 to 63 knots) are forecast for the area.

HURRICANE WARNING: Two square red flags with black centers displayed by day and a white light between two red lights at night to indicate that winds 74 miles an hour (64 knots) and above are forecast for the area.

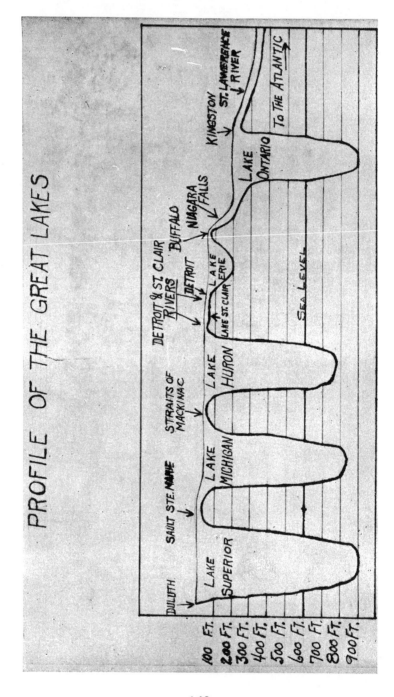

PROFILE OF THE GREAT LAKES

⚓ ⚓ ⚓ ⚓ ⚓ ⚓ ⚓ ⚓

CHAPTER TEN

THE CARAVELS OF CHRISTOPHER COLUMBUS

Santa Maria—Pinta—Nina

From a pier at the foot of East Ninth Street in Cleveland, Ohio, on an early October day in 1913, the author intently watched a most interesting sight. The tiny fleet of Christopher Columbus, in replica, was anchoring just off the pier. The view obtained must have been identical with that of the native Indians who stood on the shore of the island of San Salvador, four hundred and twenty-one years before, to the exact day, and watched those intrepid navigators maneuver their ships into position for anchorage.

The tiny *Nina* (Spanish for baby) was the first to let go her anchor, followed quickly by the somewhat larger *Pinta,* and lastly the *Santa Maria* dropped her hook on the bottom of Lake Erie. Thus the unusual fleet came in. The three caravels had just arrived from Chicago, where they had rested since the World's Fair there in 1893. They were enroute to San Francisco to be displayed at the Panama-Pacific Exposition, which was to open in that city the following year. None of the three famous caravels ever arrived at its destination, as each one met difficulty before it reached the Golden Gate.

The little fleet presented a most interesting spectacle.

161

The boats were built in the Navy Yards of Cadiz and Barcelona, Spain. The Spanish government appointed a commission, composed of naval architects and archaeologists, which spent six months in study and investigation in order to build these replicas as exactly as possible. The Spanish government stood the expense of constructing the *Santa Maria,* and the United States government paid the bills of the *Nina* and the *Pinta.*

After figuring in some Columbus festivities held at Huelva, Spain, in 1892, in which the Queen of Spain reviewed them, the little boats left Cadiz, Spain, on February 18, 1893, to follow Columbus' route across the Atlantic. The *Santa Maria* was commanded by a Spanish Navy Captain, while the *Pinta* and *Nina* were each commanded by United States Navy men. All three of the caravels were convoyed by navy vessels; the *Santa Maria* by a Spanish man-of-war; the *Pinta* by the United States Cruiser *Bennington;* and the *Nina* by the United States Cruiser *Newark.* The crews reported a very uncomfortable crossing, but about the middle of the following month, the odd fleet arrived safely in the harbor at Havana, Cuba. Here the *Pinta* and the *Nina* were, by previous arrangements, turned over to Spanish authorities, and were manned by Spanish crews. The flag of Castile and Leon, under which Columbus had sailed, flew from their mastheads.

The ancient replicas were then sailed to the United States and figured in the Naval Reviews at Norfolk, Virginia, and New York City. They were then taken to Chicago and placed on display in the World's Fair.

THE CARAVELS OF COLUMBUS

The fleet was outfitted aboard ship as nearly and completely as it was when Columbus sailed. A visit aboard the caravels was both historical and educational. The crudeness of life aboard ship in the years around 1492 could be easily visualized. There were no sea charts to follow, and none of the scientific navigating instruments of today, not even clocks to tell the time of day. A sand glass that had to be turned ever half hour was their only instrument of measuring time. Columbus did have a very crude compass which helped guide him westward across the Atlantic. The *Pinta* and the *Nina* had no decks, but the *Santa Maria* boasted of two: one, perched high in the stern of the ship, the earliest form of the poop-deck; the other, a small deck forward in the bow, the earliest form of the forecastle. As Columbus sailed his fleet, the *Nina* had a crew of twenty-four men, the *Pinta*, slightly larger, numbered thirty men. The *Santa Maria* had sixty-two sailors in her crew.

Christopher Columbus had sailed out of Palos Harbor on the morning of Friday, August 3, 1492, and, after a perilous voyage, told in every world history, sighted land on October 12, 1492. To this effort goes the credit of the discovery of the New World.

After being on display along Lake Erie, the little replica fleet continued on its way to salt water and San Francisco. However, as the boats were at that time over twenty years old, and the proposed voyage would be about four times the distance of the original cruise, the undertaking came to grief. Financial difficulties also beset the worthy venture. Eventually the three caravels were returned to Chicago, where in February, 1919, the *Nina* burned. Prior to this the *Pinta* had sunk and was left to rot. Only the flagship *Santa Maria* remains, in bad repair, in Jackson Park, Chicago.

Their long stay in the waters of the Great Lakes and the widespread interest accorded them while there, rates them as interesting ships of the Great Lakes, despite the fact that they came originally from salt water.

NOTE—The anchor of the original *Santa Maria* is on display in the Chicago Historical Society's Museum.

CHAPTER ELEVEN

SAILED AWAY

With the many modern devices for ship communication on the lakes today, it is almost impossible for a ship to encounter difficulty without word being received of her plight. However, it does happen occasionally. The steamer *Sand Merchant* was lost on the wild night of October 17, 1936, within sight of the lights of the City of Cleveland. Eighteen men and one woman perished with the wreck. She carried no radio or wireless, and no one on shore or aboard another ship saw her distress flares or sighted the flames made by burning oil-soaked rags and bedding on her steel deck. Seven men were rescued the next morning after they had clung to overturned life boats all night. They were picked up by the passing freighters *Marquette & Bessemer No. 1* and the *Thunder Bay Quarries*. They were in a state of exhaustion from their struggle to keep above the waves, but all those rescued lived.

The *Sand Merchant* was bound for Cleveland with a load of construction sand which she had sucked from the bottom of Lake Erie near Point Pelee. She left the loading spot about two P. M. with the weather ordinary for October. About 4 P. M. the wind began to rise, but caused the *Sand Merchant* crew no undue alarm. Then between eight and nine o'clock that night the gale began.

165

The wind increased until it was between forty and forty-five miles an hour, and blew from the northwest. It beat against the stern causing huge ten and twelve foot waves to thrash about the laden ship.

The ship began to take in water faster than her pumps could get rid of it. Her sand cargo sloshed around in her hold, mixing with the water. The *Sand Merchant* listed badly to port. At nine o'clock that night the ship's whistle sounded a general alarm. All hands fell to in the hope of righting the vessel before she would roll completely over, and the crew worked desperately. Her pumps were in good order, but Lake Erie was in a desperate mood and continued to wreak her wrath on the two hundred and fifty-two foot ship, then only nine years old. Over the *Sand Merchant* swept the huge waves which filled her hold; the pumps were swamped.

Captain Graham MacLelland ordered the crew into the life boats. Cleveland harbor was seventeen miles ahead, but the *Sand Merchant* was doomed never to make port. She suddenly lurched over on her side and then settled beneath the waves. The crew struggled in the darkness to keep the life boats on even keel, but to no avail. Those who had not gone down with the wreck now found themselves clinging to two overturned life boats. During the night, several of these men, unable to hang onto the unwieldy overturned life boats, slid to their deaths beneath the roaring waves.

Shortly after dawn the next day, the rescue ships, leaving Cleveland for upper lake ports, found the survivors still clinging to the overturned life boats. Exhausted, they were brought aboard and made comfortable and taken ashore for hospitalization. Practically no wreckage came ashore from the *Sand Merchant* and, were it not for a few survivors and their rescue, the story of the tragedy might never have been known. All this in the year 1936 and within sight of the lights of Cleveland!

The *Sand Merchant* still rests on the bottom of the lake. She went down out of the traffic lanes and is not a menace. No attempts have been made to raise the vessel.

Many ships have sailed away on the Great Lakes never to be heard of again. Here are the stories in brief of some of them.

On January 21, 1895, the passenger steamer *Chicora* left Milwaukee for St. Joseph, Michigan. Nothing was ever seen of the ship; very little wreckage and no bodies were ever found. Lake Michigan swallowed the *Chicora* and left no crumbs. Twenty-six lives were lost.

Lake Superior has its "Flying Dutchman" even as does salt water. The "Flying Dutchman" of the ocean is a

Dutch ship that mysteriously disappeared, leaving no trace. Superstitious sailors claim to have sighted the old Dutchman on wild nights at sea, weirdly riding the waves. Such a ship is the *Bannockburn,* a freighter, lost on Lake Superior with twenty-two men aboard. She sailed from Duluth one early winter morning and was sighted by a passing ship the following evening. That was the last seen of the *Bannockburn.* A year and a half later, an oar was found on the Michigan shore—the only thing ever reported from the ill-fated ship. Through wind-swept pilot house windows, in the dead of a wild night, lake sailors say they have sighted the *Bannockburn* sailing serenely over the tempestuous waves, never again to reach port.

Years ago the steamer *Alpena* was sighted by passing ships about thirty miles from Chicago in Lake Michigan. She never made port and was never heard from again.

In December, 1909, the four-year-old carferry *Marquette & Bessemer No. 2,* loaded a string of railroad cars at Conneaut, Ohio, for Port Stanley, Ontario, across Lake Erie. All being well and the ship in good shape, the *Marquette & Bessemer* cleared the Conneaut breakwater, never to be seen again. The big carferry disappeared completely. Thirty-six men in her crew went to watery graves.

A shipbuilding concern at Fort William, Ontario, built two mine sweepers for the French Government, completing the ships in 1918. Hoping to get them through the lakes and into salt water before the ice closed the lakes to navigation, the two sweepers, the *Cerisoler* and the *Inkerman*, sailed from their builder's plant one month before Christmas endeavoring to make Kingston, Ontario, their first stop. The twin ships never left Lake Superior. They were never reported as reaching the Sault Ste. Marie locks, through which all ships leaving Lake Superior must go, to get into Lake Huron and the lower lakes. They were lost without a trace in Lake Superior. No wreckage has ever been reported from them, nor have any of the bodies of the seventy-six men aboard the two vessels ever been seen.

On December 21, 1922, the tug *Cornell* left Cleveland bound for Buffalo. She sailed away into eternity. Although some bodies were later found, no one will ever know just what happened to cause the stout tug to disappear so mysteriously.

169

LORE OF THE LAKES

The tale of the five hundred ton, one hundred eighty foot, three - masted schooner *Rouse Simmons* is tragic indeed. Years ago, just before Christmas, it was the custom to cut Christmas trees in the north woods, load them onto schooners, and ship them into the large cities on the lakes for market. Such was the cargo of the *Simmons* as she sailed under Captain J. Schuneman from Thompson Harbor, near Manistique, Michigan, at noon on November 25th, 1913. The lakes were still giving up their wreckage from the "Big Storm" of that year, when the schooner, with sail set, cleared the port into a raging gale, bound for Chicago. Time was short, and if the trees were to reach the market, the *Simmons* had to crowd all possible speed. Winter in all its fury beat upon the little ship as she forced her way up Lake Michigan. Ice formed fast.

Off Point Aux Barque, the crew of the tug *Burger*, which was also battling the gale and towing the schooner *Dutch Boy*, sighted the Christmas tree laden craft. To their astonishment, they saw the *Simmons* head into the open lake, while they were doing their utmost to reach port and safety. Evidently Captain Schuneman wanted to be a safe distance from shore, preferring the open lake to being blown against the land.

Next morning at dawn, the *Simmons* was again sighted about 100 miles from where she was last seen, this time by the Coast Guardsmen off Sturgeon Bay, during a lull in the howling snow storm which had come up during the night. The *Simmons* was now flying distress signals, but the guardsmen were unable to aid the little ship in its sorry plight. They phoned the Coast Guard Station at

Kewaunee, Wisconsin, in which direction the *Simmons* was headed.

The Kewaunee guardsmen put out immediately in a search that, for a long time, was futile. Suddenly, during a lull in the falling snow, they sighted the distressed schooner. Her sails were in tatters and her rigging, hull and cabins were heavily coated with ice. The sturdy life-savers headed for her, but before they had covered half of the distance, the snow set in again and the schooner vanished. That was the last ever seen of the *Rouse Simmons*. Seventeen persons were believed to have been aboard and all were lost.

The following spring, fishermen from Two Rivers, Wisconsin, reported finding Christmas trees in their nets. It was thought they were from that holiday cargo of the ill-fated little ship.

Land, part of the State of Michigan, juts northward into Lake Superior. It is called the Keweenaw Peninsula. Here are located the rich deposits of copper. The peninsula curves slightly to the east and forms a protected bay between itself and the south shore of the lake. This is called Keweenaw Bay, and where it narrows into the land at its head is located the town of Baraga. Baraga was a lumber shipping port in years gone by, and many an old lumber "hooker" loaded its cargo of the forest product there for delivery to the lower lake ports. Many of the sturdy wooden steamers pulled tows of one or two barges, their decks also heavily laden with lumber.

Captain J. P. Jennings of Detroit had brought the lumber steamer *C. F. Curtis,* towing the barges *Annie M. Peterson* and *Seldon E. Marvin,* into Baraga to load lumber for delivery to Tonawanda, New York. Aboard the three vessels were twenty-six men; two women, one a cook and the other a stewardess, were on the *Curtis.*

The *C. F. Curtis* was a powerful little ship and well able to handle the two tows in almost any weather. She was one hundred ninety-six feet long and had been built in 1882. The *Annie M. Peterson* had once been a sailing schooner, but her tall masts and spars had been removed with the coming of dependable steamers and she had been converted into a barge. She was larger than the one hundred seventy-five foot *Seldon E. Marvin,* which had been built in 1881 as a barge. For this reason the *Marvin* was usually the end boat in the tow, with the *Peterson* between it and the *Curtis.*

Captain John Walker was in command of the *Peterson* and Captain Fred E. Anderson, of Chicago, was master of the *Marvin.* The three ships were reported as being owned by the Edward Hines Lumber Company, Chicago.

It was Wednesday, the eighteenth of November, 1914, that the trio finished loading and Captain Jennings, anxious to get started, cast off his lines and assembled his tows for the long trip to Tonawanda, near Buffalo, almost the entire length of the Great Lakes. The lumber "hooker" and her two consorts were off on what was destined to be their last cruise! Not one of the persons aboard the three ships would live to tell the tale!

Out onto Keweenaw Bay they sailed. As they rounded Point Abbaye into Lake Superior all was well and the course was set for Whitefish Point, some one hundred and fifty miles eastward. The shore line on their starboard faded from sight as the three boats plowed their way along. On their port side extended the vast reaches of the cold tumbling waters of Lake Superior.

Just what happened after that can only be pieced together by lake men familiar with these waters. Night came on and with it a howling blizzard. The boats carried no wireless. Ice formed fast from the spray of the waves that beat against the struggling ships. Snow blotted out everything. It is believed that all of the next day, Thursday, they battled the gale and that during that night they met their end.

Somehow their towing lines parted and the barges wallowed helplessly on the raging lake. No one ship could see either of the others because of the thick swirling snow. Probably their cargoes shifted. Undoubtedly the waves swept mercilessly over their decks.

On Friday, the bodies of six men and two women, all frozen stiff, along with considerable wreckage from the *Curtis* and the *Peterson,* were found on the south shore of Lake Superior, eight miles from Grand Marais, Michigan. For several days the wreckage and bodies washed ashore. Two men lived to reach land and, unseen by anyone, made their way toward safety. They never reached

173

it, as the intense cold overcame them and they were later found frozen to death some distance from the water's edge. Not a soul survived the disaster! Large fields of lumber, along with wreckage from both boats, floated ashore.

The next day word came from forty miles farther east of Grand Marais that wreckage from the *Marvin* was found on the shore. Evidently the *Marvin* outlived the other two boats and had been blown along in the storm, only to be wrecked later. Records indicate that only wreckage and cargo, but no bodies, ever came ashore from the *Marvin*. About eighteen bodies were recovered from the *Curtis* and the *Peterson*.

About one week later the revenue cutter *Mackinac,* which was cruising about the scene of the disaster, located the bow of the *Marvin* floating low in the water. There was nothing else left of the ill-fated barge. The *Mackinac* towed the derelict to shore and beached it there, out of the way of other and more fortunate vessels.

Captain Hudson of the Canadian steamer *Glencairn* found broken hatch covers floating in the middle of Lake Huron on Saturday, September 27th, in 1924. All ships had been requested to watch for wreckage of the steamer *Clifton,* which was then many days overdue at Detroit. Nothing had been seen nor heard of the *Clifton* since she had passed through the Straits of Mackinac, downbound, at 10:20 Sunday morning, September 21st.

174

SAILED AWAY

The *Clifton* had joined that fleet of missing ships that had sailed away and failed to reach port. Later, Captain Hudson saw the forward part of a pilot house floating on the lake. He had the wreckage brought aboard the *Glencairn* and identified it as part of the missing *Clifton*. Fastened securely to part of the pilot house were the ship's searchlight and clock, which had stopped at 4 o'clock.

Since a storm had been at the height of its fury during the early morning hours of Monday, September 22nd, marine men figured that that was the day and hour that the *Clfton* had plunged to the bottom with its entire crew and cargo of crushed stone. The twenty-eight men comprising her crew had perished.

The *Clifton* was of the whaleback or "pig" type of lake ship, built in 1892, and was three hundred and eight feet keel, thirty feet beam, twenty-four feet depth and a capacity of thirty-five hundred tons. She was formerly the *Samuel Mather*. During the winter of 1923-24 she had been converted into a self-unloader. She is reported to have been owned by the Progress Steamship Company of Cleveland. Her master was Captain Emmett Gallagher of St. James, Beaver Island, Michigan.

The *Clifton* had loaded crushed stone at Sturgeon Bay, Wisconsin, and had sailed from there on Saturday, September 20th, bound for Detroit. A bad blow had swept Lake Huron after the *Clifton* had entered that lake and most steamers had sought shelter. As the hours dragged into days and nothing was heard from the *Clifton*, fears for her safety arose. Seaplanes were sent to scour the

175

lake to locate the missing vessel, but they returned with no word. It was exactly one week from the day the *Clifton* left Sturgeon Bay that the *Glencairn* found her wreckage floating in Lake Huron.

What caused the *Clifton* to disappear is still a mystery. Did her unloading boom tear loose from its fastenings and thrash violently about on the pitching boat? Did it swing far out over the side and cause the ship to roll over and sink? No one will ever know exactly, as all the crew were lost and the wreck was never located.

There is very little to tell of the mysterious disappearance of the Canadian package freighter *Kamloops*. Lake Superior swallowed the ship one day in early December in 1927, and from all available records there has never been anything further seen or heard of the ill-fated ship.

That winter caught many of the lake boats fast in the ice in the St. Mary's River below the Soo locks. Captain Fred Bailey was in charge of the ice breaking operations and his efforts were being closely watched by the anxious men of the lakes. The *Kamloops* had passed through the river, upbound, a few days ahead of the "big freeze" and had locked through the canal and headed her prow toward Fort William, Ontario.

Directly ahead of her, and in plain sight, was the Canadian steamer *Quedoc*, also heading for the same port.

SAILED AWAY

A strong northwest gale bearing heavy snow flurries whirled down upon the two ships. The temperature fell fast. At Duluth it registered eighteen below zero; at Fort William it was ten below; while at the Soo it held at two below. The two freighters battled the wind, waves and intense cold on their lonely trek across the big lake. Frequently they were lost to sight of each other as the snow would swirl about them. Suddenly Isle Royale appeared dead ahead of the leading ship, the *Quedoc*. Fast work was required to avoid having the ship stranded on its icy shore. This action occupied the entire attention of the crew and, when their danger was past, they looked back to see the *Kamloops*.

But the *Kamloops* was not to be seen! Nor has she ever been seen since! Twenty men and two women cooks went down with their ship. Truly, the *Kamloops* had joined the list of ships that had "sailed away."

"S. S. Milwaukee,"
"Oct. 22,-'29, 6:30 P. M."
"Ship is taking water fast. We have turned and headed for Milwaukee. Pumps are all working, but sea-gate is bent and won't keep water out. Flickers are flooded. Seas are tremendous. Things look bad. Crew roll about same as last pay day."
(Signed) "A. R. Sadon, Purser."

At South Haven, Michigan, the Coast Guards found a battered can floating near the beach. It contained this note. The writing was in pencil and the can had leaked, making the words almost illegible. About a week earlier, on Tuesday, October 22nd, the Grand Trunk carferry *Milwaukee* had steamed out of the harbor at Milwaukee with twenty-seven box cars, each loaded with freight, for its destination, Muskegon, Michigan, on the opposite side of Lake Michigan.

The *Milwaukee* carried no wireless equipment. She was in seaworthy condition. Built in 1903 at Cleveland, the ship, a twin screw propeller, was three hundred and thirty-eight feet long and fifty-two feet beam. Fifty-two persons comprised the crew.

The freight cars were run aboard the vessel on special tracks equipped with clamps to keep the cars from shifting while the ship was in motion. One of those infrequent gales blew across the lake and whipped the waves into tremendous towering walls of water which beat upon the luckless carferry furiously. Evidently, according to Purser Sadon's note, they smashed the sea-gate at the vessel's stern, so that it could not keep out the water.

The carferry had sailed about noon. During the afternoon the storm increased in fury. Evidently, the captain tried to return to Milwaukee. At 6:30 that night Purser Sadon wrote his tragic note and cast it upon the raging waters, fearing that no other word of their plight might ever be told, and hoping his little can would be found. After that, things probably happened fast aboard the storm-tossed stricken ship.

SAILED AWAY

It is presumed that the freight cars tore loose from their fastenings and rolled about on their tracks, thereby shifting the weight of the cargo, and, with the ship already taking water badly, she sank. All this is surmised, as not a soul ever lived to tell what actually happened out there on Lake Michigan on that wild night aboard the *Milwaukee*.

Reports show that some days later the freighter *Colonel*, of the Cleveland Cliffs fleet, found wreckage from the ill-fated carferry floating in Lake Michigan. All hopes for the safety of the *Milwaukee* ended with the finding of the wreckage. Thus did the *Milwaukee* add her name to that fleet of lake vessels that had "sailed away."

These are the tragic stories of some of the outstanding ships that have sailed away from ports on the Great Lakes, never to be heard from again. Fresh water "Flying Dutchmen" all!

♒ ♒ ♒ ♒ ♒ ♒ ♒ ♒

Chapter Twelve

THE TASHMOO AND CITY OF ERIE RACE

In the very early morning of June 4th, 1901, intense activity prevailed on the decks of the Cleveland & Buffalo Transit Company's crack lake liner, *City of Erie*. The ship had just arrived in Cleveland that morning on her regular run from Buffalo and was at her dock in the Cuyahoga River. Passengers were hurriedly sent ashore and the stevedores broke all unloading records placing her freight cargo on the dock.

This was the day for the big race with the steamer *Tashmoo*, of Detroit, affectionately called "The White Flyer" and the pride of its owners, The White Star Line.

The weather for the event was perfect. Lake Erie outdid herself to provide ideal sailing conditions; the surface was smooth; there was only a whiff of a breeze; the sky was a clear azure blue without a cloud.

The docks and offices ashore were alive with people milling about. Aboard ship, the genial skipper, Captain Hugh McAlpine, hurried the already rushing crew into stowing the lifeboats on the lower deck to avoid their resistance to the wind and her flagpoles were removed for the same reason.

In the engine room there was the scene of sweating men hurriedly checking their engines, making certain that all was in readiness. Chief Engineer Rendall was careful that nothing should fail. The firemen below decks were sorting coal, discarding any pieces that looked stony and might cause clinkers under her huge boilers. Every man in her crew had wagered his all on that race. In those days a man stood by his ship always, with all he had, and in this case, with all he could borrow.

The general public, ever ready for a sporting event, was lining the lake front to catch a glimpse of the ships as they sped eastward. Detroiters and folks from along the St. Clair and Detroit Rivers were among the crowd and their bets showed their faith in their champion, the sleek river speed queen, *Tashmoo*. Many Detroiters chartered the passenger steamer *Frank E. Kirby* and watched the race from that ship. Ohioans supported strongly the *City of Erie*. Largely, it was Detroit vs. Cleveland, with everyone else interested.

The course to be run was straight along the south shore of Lake Erie, starting from a line off the waterworks crib, six miles outside of the breakwater at Cleveland, to a line ten miles off Presque Isle lighthouse at Erie, Pennsylvania. The distance was almost one hundred miles. The nearest point of land to the racing course was at Fairport, Ohio, where the ships would pass about two and one-half miles off shore. There, business was suspended for the day and the schools closed, as everyone went to the waterfront to be on hand for the greatest marine sporting event ever to be held on the Great Lakes.

Great care was taken to make the affair satisfactory and decisive. Reputable and impartial judges and time-keepers were selected and agreed upon. Among these were Captain Charles L. Hutchinson, John A. Donaldson, Percy W. Rice, Waldo A. Avery and Arnold C. Saunders, all well known lake marine men. Government inspectors were present to see that no infractions of the law occurred. Two lanes were mapped out on the course so that the racing steamers were always at least half a mile apart, broadside, from the start to the finish, the lanes being marked by buoys and small boats anchored along the course.

The choice of position was decided by lot, the *Tashmoo* winning and wisely choosing the outer course. This gave her a bit deeper water than her rival, in some of the stretches, which added some to her speed. The day before the great race the *Tashmoo* had steamed gracefully into Cleveland harbor and spent the night behind the breakwater. She was in charge of Captain B. S. Baker, well known Detroit skipper.

The *City of Erie* proceeded slowly down the narrow Cuyahoga River, from her dock to the open lake, to meet the *Tashmoo* and to start the big marine race. It is quite unlikely that another such race between large steamboats will ever be run on the Great Lakes. Due to the risk involved, the government officials frown on such affairs, and owners dislike to submit their ships to the strain entailed, to say nothing of the additional expense. The practical side dominates the emotional. Therefore, the exciting spectacle of two giant steamers splitting the water side by side for one hundred miles, their stacks belching forth volumes of black smoke and their sidewheels churning the water into flying foam, as they speed onward to their goal, will likely never be seen again. It can only be re-lived in narrative, by those who were fortunate enough to witness the stirring scene.

The two vessels worked abreast of each other as they approached the starting line and each shut off her engines as they neared it. It was a few minutes past nine-thirty. Boom! The little cannon on the tug boat at the starting line sounded the start of the race. Bells clanged sharply aboard the rival steamers, their paddle wheels started churning the water as their sharp prows crossed the line. They were off to a good start.

Harbor craft blew their whistles and factories ashore took up the salutations until complete bedlam prevailed. The records show that the *City of Erie* crossed the starting line just a few seconds ahead of the *Tashmoo*. The *Tashmoo,* however, slowly pulled abreast of the *City of Erie* and the two ships continued neck-and-neck for about one hour. Huge swells from the wash of the racing vessels surged up on the distant shore, testifying to the tremendous driving energy that was called forth by the ships as they crowded their engines to their utmost. Clouds of smoke, steam and spray followed them in the air.

As they neared Fairport the *Tashmoo* slowly forged ahead of its rival. First one ship's length, then another, and still another. Hearts sank aboard the *City of Erie.*

"Never mind. Just wait until we are past this shoal water and then see what we'll do when we strike that deep water," said Captain McAlpine, as he scanned the lake's smooth deeper blue surface ahead.

He was right! As the shoal water was left astern, the *City of Erie* began to shorten the distance between it and the *Tashmoo*. As the racers sped past Ashtabula Harbor, the *City of Erie* pulled abreast of the *Tashmoo* once more. From then on it was the *City of Erie's* race. She slowly but surely forged ahead and as Conneaut was passed she was about two lengths ahead of the *Tashmoo*. Twenty miles from the finish line found the *City of Erie* a scant three lengths in the lead. From this point until they crossed the finish line off Erie, both ships held this same position. On and on they flashed through the water, neither ship gaining nor losing any appreciable distance.

The officials in the timekeepers' and judges' boats that marked the finish line were tossed about in the turbulent swells as the two giant racers shot past them. But their stop watches had recorded the excitingly close finish. The prow of the *City of Erie* had crossed the line just forty-five seconds ahead of that of the *Tashmoo!*

The *Tashmoo*, after ascertaining that she had definitely lost by so close a margin, saluted the winner in true good sportsmanship. Both vessels then turned about, amidst a din of steam whistles from other steamers at the finish line, and returned to Cleveland at a less exciting and strenuous pace.

The great lake classic had been run and new speed records were set up; records that to present writing are somewhat enviable by any passenger ship, although some of the newest steamers can better the old race time.

Much has happened aboard ship since this famous race at the beginning of the century. The wireless was not dreamed of by these sailors, neither were airplanes, news reels, radio, ship-to-shore telephones, and many other everyday safety devices that protect and aid the ships of today.

The newspaper reporters, aboard the racing vessels, assigned to cover the event, were greatly handicapped in getting their reports of the race ashore and into their editorial rooms. They used the lowly pigeon to carry their latest reports. As one ship or the other would change position, the reporters would scribble the news on a small tissue paper, fasten it to the bird's leg and turn him loose to flutter and fly out over the water to his home nest. Once there, eager hands relieved him of his burden and hurried the message on to the newspapers' headquarters.

Another method used by the reporters was to toss overboard their message, sealed in a tin can, to a waiting small boat at predetermined spots along the route of the race. This message was then hurried ashore and relayed to headquarters. The only way the watchers ashore at the finish line at Erie knew for certain which ship actually won the race, was by a prearranged signal from the judges' boat. This was three kites flung aloft in the summer breeze. Thus did the world ashore learn that the *City of Erie* had won the race.

For the reader who is interested in statistics pertaining to this grand old race, the following data may prove of interest.

STATISTICS OF TASHMOO-CITY OF ERIE RACE

	City of Erie	Tashmoo
Year built	1898	·1900
Length over all, feet	324	308
Length on keel, feet	314	300
Beam, feet	44	37.5
Breadth over guards, feet	77.2	69
Depth, feet	18	13.5
Draft, forward, feet	9.75	8.12
Draft, aft, feet	10.83	8.46
Draft, mean, feet	10.29	8.29
Displacement, tons	2,233	1,224
Trial load, tons	250	60
Wetted surface, sq. ft.	12,776	8,976
Prismatic coefficient	.603	.584
Engine type	Compound Beam	Triple Inclined

DATA OF THE RUN

	City of Erie	Tashmoo
Steam pressure, pounds	120.4	175*
Vacuum, inches	23.4	22
Air pressure, inches	5 max.	
Revolutions per minute	33.25	40.08
M. E. P. in H. P. cylinder, pounds	58.4	
I. P. cylinder, pounds		
L. P. cylinder, pounds	36.6	
Distance, in statute miles	94	94
Speed in statute miles per hour	21.76	21.70
Speed, in knots per hour	18.899	18.847
Slip of wheel over bucket, %	35.65	32.2
Depth of water in feet, start	57	57
minimum	35	35
maximum	77	77
average	61.31	61.31
Admiralty coefficient	178.2	225

Note: *L. P. pass over valve half open during last 1½ hours.

(Detailed information courtesy of Mr. C. B. Percy of Detroit.)

THE TASHMOO AND CITY OF ERIE RACE

JUDGES' REPORT

On Board Stmr. City of Erie
   June 4th, 1901
To the owners of Steamer Tashmoo
        and
Steamer City of Erie
Gentlemen:

We as judges appointed by you to decide race between Cleveland and Erie, beg to report results as follows:

		Hours	Minutes	Seconds
City of Erie left Cleveland	A. M.	9	37	56
Arrived in Erie	P. M.	1	57	05
Time of City of Erie		4	19	09
Steamer Tashmoo left Cleveland	A. M.	9	38	31
Arrived at Erie	P. M.	1	58	25
Time of Tashmoo		4	19	54
Time of Tashmoo		4	19	54
Time of City of Erie		4	19	09

Difference of time in favor of City of Erie, in seconds.................. 45

All conditions being favorable to both boats, we consider this one of the fairest races of the kind ever made and we therefore declare that the steamer City of Erie is the winner of the race.

(Signed) Percy W. Rice,
Waldo A. Avery,
Arnold C. Saunders.

Today, almost forty years after the big Lake Erie race, the grand old steamer *City of Erie* lies at a dock in Cleveland, awaiting its next uncertain move. She made her last trip for the old C & B Line between Buffalo and Cleveland in the fall of 1937. That winter she was moored alongside her sister ship, the *City of Buffalo,* at East Ninth Street Pier in Cleveland.

In March, 1938, the *City of Buffalo* caught fire and was destroyed. The *City of Erie* escaped the flames. What the future holds for the old "Honeymoon Special" is anyone's guess.

The trim white *Tashmoo* has vanished completely from the lakes. No more will her sonorous whistle echo over the waters. Gone is that source of pleasure for those

187

Detroiters who used to gather on her decks and enjoy a day's outing on the water. The wreckers' tools have torn the sleek vessel apart.

Her last trip was made from Detroit down the river, on an evening ride, on June 18, 1936. She had on board about fourteen hundred passengers. Many were dancing. In the darkness the *Tashmoo* hit an obstruction, believed to have been a loose rock in the channel, and a gaping hole was torn in her hull, below the water line.

She was headed immediately for the nearest dock, which happened to be at Amherstberg, on the Canadian side of the Detroit River. With her orchestra still playing and her passengers still dancing, apparently unaware of the situation, the ship was rushed to the dock. The passengers were all safely landed and a major lake disaster was thus narrowly averted.

The *Tashmoo* sank at the dock soon after arriving, in about fifteen feet of water. Her upper decks were still well above the water's surface. It was eventually decided to abandon the ship to the wreckers, and so ended the career of the famous Detroit pleasure boat.

Her ship's bell now hangs on display in the Ford Museum at Dearborn, Michigan, and many a Detroiter stands before it and recalls how its strokes signaled the happy start of a day's holiday for him aboard the old vessel. It is reported that her pilot house, bridge and master's quarters were removed all in one piece and sent to a spot near the St. Clair Flats, where they now serve as a unique summer residence.

Chapter Thirteen

THE BIG STORM

Any lake sailorman who was aboard a ship on the days of Sunday, Monday, Tuesday and Wednesday of November 9th, 10th, 11th and 12th in the year of 1913, knows these are exactly the days of the Big Storm. No other storm has in any way ever approached that one. It was the most disastrous that has ever swept our Great Lakes, both from loss of life and property.

The story of misery, anxiety, suffering, loss and damage caused on the lakes by the Big Storm will never be completely told. Only the high spots stand out in the fateful records of the many ill-destined ships that encountered that hurricane and lost. Records vary as to the exact number of lake vessels that did not survive. Accounting for the many craft lost is a matter of personal opinion depending on the viewpoint, such as: whether or not the ship was a total wreck, or could later be salvaged; whether the vessel was large enough to be classed as a ship; whether a stranding is to be classed as a lost ship; and many other details.

Some authorities claim as high as thirty-two boats were wrecked and two hundred and fifty men and women perished in the blow. However, most lake men agree that eleven freighters were a total loss through sinking and

189

stranding, and six or seven more were wrecked badly enough to be judged by the underwriters as total losses. The actual loss in dollars will never be known. Fortunately, few passenger ships were caught in the storm, as the season for passenger travel was practically over. Lucky indeed were the sailors who brought their battered ships into port after being buffeted about by the Big Storm.

Usually a storm on the lakes is nothing to deter the crews of the staunch lake freighters. True, they are not welcomed, but schedules must be maintained and the ships must plow through the heavy seas, seeking shelter only when extreme danger threatens. Thus it was on that Saturday, November 8th, of that year the lake shipping battled what started to be just another early winter blow. Captains then had no way of knowing that this blow was going to be worse than any other that they had ever encountered.

"No lake master can recall in all his experience," reported the Lake Carriers Association afterwards, "a storm of such unprecedented violence with such rapid changes in the direction of the wind and its gusts of such fearful speed. Storms ordinarily of that velocity do not last over four or five hours, but this storm raged for sixteen hours continuously at an average velocity of sixty miles per hour, with frequent spurts of seventy and over.

"Obviously with a wind of such long duration, the seas that were made were such that the lakes are not ordinarily familiar with. The testimony of masters is that the waves were at least thirty-five feet high and followed each other in quick succession, three waves ordinarily coming one right after the other.

"They were considerably shorter than the waves that are formed by the ordinary gale. Being of such height and hurled with such force and such rapid succession, the ships must have been subjected to incredible punishment.

"Masters also relate that the wind and sea were frequently in conflict, the wind blowing one way and the sea running in the opposite direction. This would indicate a storm of cyclonic character. It was unusual and unprecedented and it may be centuries before such a combination of forces may be experienced again."

In the big cities that border the lakes, and throughout the surrounding country, land traffic was paralyzed. Communication and power lines were wrecked. Street and interurban cars were left stranded in the streets, stalled by the snow and the ice that formed on the wires and rails. Thousands of persons were marooned in whatever shelter they could find while the storm raged. Railroads abandoned trying to operate their trains. But to the men aboard ships on the lakes it was stark tragedy.

Little of what went on aboard the ships that were lost is known. There were no survivors to tell the story of horror. It can only be gleaned from the wreckage and from those sailors on ships fortunate enough to make port.

Newspapers carried long lists of the boats hit by the gale. One such list included the following vessels:

Regina, missing.

Wexford, missing.

James Carruthers, Canada's biggest grain boat. Wreckage washed ashore near Goderich, Ontario.

Huronic, aground off Whitefish Point. Crew and passengers safe.

L. C. Waldo, stranded on rocks at Gull Rock, Manitou Island, in Lake Superior. Twenty-two crew members rescued, no lives lost. Vessel a total loss.

Wm. Nottingham, stranded on Parisian Island near Point Arthur, Ontario.

Turret Chief, driven ashore six miles north of Copper Harbor, Michigan. Lifted high on beach by gale; crew rescued after suffering intense cold.

Matthew Andrews, aground on Corsica Shoal in lower Lake Huron, near Port Huron.

H. M. Hanna, ashore near Point Aux Barques, Lake Huron.

Matoa, ashore near Point Aux Barques, Lake Huron. Ship probably a total loss.

J. M. Jenks, ashore in Georgian Bay near Midland, Ontario.

A. E. Stewart, aground in Whitefish Bay, Lake Superior.

F. G. Hartwell, in difficulty in Whitefish Bay with ore cargo. Crew taken off.

Acadian, aground on a reef near Sulphur Island in Lake Superior.

Robert Fulton, aground at Bar Point in Lake Erie. Later released.

THE BIG STORM

U. S. Lightship No. 61, blown ashore at head of St. Clair River.

U. S. Lightship No. 82, missing from her station in Lake Erie, between Point Abino and Sturgeon Point, near Buffalo.

John T. Hutchinson, ashore at Point Iroquois in Lake Superior.

Northern Queen, ashore near Kettle Point in Lake Huron. Crew rescued, but steamer probably a total loss.

Barge *Plymouth,* in difficulty off St. Martin's Island in Lake Michigan, with seven men aboard.

D. O. Mills, ashore at Harbor Beach, Michigan. Vessel released herself.

H. B. Hawgood, ashore on Corsica Shoal, just above Point Edward, at lower end of Lake Huron. No lives lost.

Leafield, missing on Lake Superior.

Hardwick, aground near Port Huron, Michigan.

Saxona, aground in the St. Clair River. Released herself.

Victory, aground in the Livingstone Channel near Detroit. Lightened part of cargo and was released.

Thistle, small steamer, grain laden, ashore at Calumet Harbor, Michigan.

G. J. Grammer, beached one-half mile east of harbor entrance at Lorain, Ohio. Crew rescued.

Barge *Halstead,* aground near Green Bay, Wisconsin. Her crew of six missing.

Louisiana, Cleveland owned coal steamer, reported to have sunk off Washington Island in Lake Michigan. Crew of fifteen saved.

Major, wooden steamer, sprung leak and abandoned thirty miles off Whitefish Point in Lake Superior. Later towed by steamer *Barnum* to Whitefish Point.

Tug *La Fayette,* missing.

Many conflicting reports were made about various vessels and, due to the communication service being badly crippled, it required many days after the Big Storm subsided for vesselmen to actually count their lost ships.

The list of the eleven ships that were lost in the Big Storm is as follows:

Argus, sank in Lake Huron—25 lost.
James Carruthers, sank in Lake Huron—22 lost.
Hydrus, sank in Lake Huron—25 lost.
Leafield, sank in Lake Superior—18 lost.
John A. McGean, sank in Lake Huron—23 lost.
Charles S. Price, sank in Lake Huron—28 lost.
Regina, sank in Lake Huron—25 lost.
Isaac M. Scott, sank in Lake Huron—28 lost.
Henry B. Smith, sank in Lake Superior—25 lost.
Wexford, sank in Lake Huron—24 lost.
Lightship No. 82, wrecked at Buffalo—6 lost.

Outstanding among others that were wrecked were the ships:

Wm. Nottingham, ashore in Whitefish Bay—3 lost.

Howard M. Hanna (former) ashore in Lake Huron—no lives lost.

L. C. Waldo, ashore on Manitou Island, Lake Superior—no lives lost.

The freighter *Argus* was in command of Captain Paul

Gutch of Cleveland, and belonged in the fleet of the Inter-
lake Steamship Company. She was formerly the *Lewis
Woodruff* of the Gilchrist fleet. She foundered in Lake
Huron with all hands during the Big Storm. Bodies of
her crew were washed on the beach near Kincardine,
Ontario.

A new ship was the *James Carruthers*, on her third trip,
which the Big Storm decreed was also to be her last trip.
She was of Canadian registry and was bound down the
lakes with a cargo of grain when the gale reached out its
ugly arm and struck her down. A few bodies and a small
bit of wreckage was all that was found of this brand
new steamer.

The freighter *Hydrus* was in the Interlake Steamship
Company fleet and met her doom by foundering in Lake
Huron during the Big Storm. Her entire crew perished
with the ship.

The *Leafield* was a Canadian ship, owned by the
Algoma Central Steamship Line, and had been built in
Scotland for ocean travel. She was engaged in the grain
trade on the lakes when the Big Storm swooped down
on the sturdy ship and sent her crashing on the rocks of
Angus Island in Lake Superior, fourteen miles southeast
of Fort William, Ontario. Her entire crew of eighteen
perished in the icy waters.

The big freighter *John A. McGean*, of the Hutchinson
fleet, under command of Captain C. R. Ney of Cleveland,
who had sailed the lakes for thirty years, had loaded coal
at Sandusky, Ohio, and had sailed at nine-thirty Saturday
night bound for South Chicago. She was but five years
old, having been built at Lorain, Ohio, in 1908. Her

length was four hundred and thirty-two feet and beam fifty-two feet, and was of five thousand two hundred tons. While up bound in Lake Huron she foundered with all hands.

What happened to the *Charles S. Price*, an ore carrier of the Hanna fleet, and to the *Regina*, a Canadian package freighter, will always be an outstanding mystery of the Great Lakes. The two ships were last sighted close together, each desperately battling to keep afloat in the Big Storm. Another steamer, the *Wexford*, of the Western Steamship Company, Ltd., was also struggling along in the same vicinity. All three vessels were doomed.

A few miles from Fort Gratiot Light near Port Huron at the entrance to the St. Clair River on the Monday of the Big Storm, was sighted a ship floating upside down. Only the bottom of her bow extended above water. There was no way to identify her. For several days while the storm raged it floated about, unknown. When the seas subsided enough to permit a diver to go down to her, it was found that she was the *Charles S. Price*. Twenty-eight men, her entire crew, had been dumped into Lake Huron. All were lost.

The bodies of her master, Captain W. A. Black, and half of her crew were found the next day. Some of the bodies identified as from the crew of the *Price* were wearing life belts bearing the name *Regina*. There is the mystery of the Big Storm. How did the crew of one ship gain access to the life belts of another ship? What occurred in that blinding snow filled gale over the water that caused the crews to meet?

THE BIG STORM

Lake men believe that possibly the two ships may have collided in the raging hurricane and that the sailors jumped or were thrown from one ship to the other, and, seeing disaster and death facing them, hurriedly donned the nearest available life belts. But only Lake Huron knows the real answer and that is buried deep in the sands at the bottom of the lake.

The trim freighter *Isaac M. Scott* was loaded with coal and was bound for Milwaukee, when in Lake Huron the Big Storm swept tons of icy water over the ship faster than it could be pumped out, and she sank to the bottom carrying with her the entire crew and cargo.

The big steamer *Henry B. Smith,* in command of Captain James Owen, and bound from Marquette, Michigan, to the lower lakes with iron ore was lost with all hands, somewhere between Marquette and the Soo. Never has Lake Superior divulged exactly where the *Smith* met her doom.

The steamer *L. C. Waldo,* with a cargo of iron ore, sailed from Two Harbors, Minnesota, bound for Cleveland, Captain John Duddleson in command. As the *Waldo* proceeded down Lake Superior the storm increased. First, it smashed in her pilot house windows, then it took off the roof of the pilot house. Her electric light system was put out of commission. Then her compass was demolished. Huge combers flung themselves completely over the ship, but still the master and crew struggled on. They hoped to reach the shelter of Manitou Island.

So great were her handicaps and so difficult to handle

was the ship, that, during the blinding snow storm, in the dead of the night, the *Waldo* ran upon Gull Rock of the island where she was seeking shelter. The ship broke in two. How the crew lived in the after part of the ship, starving and freezing, makes a thrilling tale. The next day the steamer *Lakeland* saw her plight. Fortunately, she carried wireless equipment, a scarcely used apparatus in those days on the lakes. She broadcast the situation of the *Waldo*. Help came from two directions, the Coast Guard stations at Portage and at Eagle Harbor. They rescued the crew just as the food supply was exhausted. Gold medals of honor were awarded each of the Coast Guard stations making the rescue.

Bodies of the men aboard the *Wexford*, a Canadian ship, were washed ashore on the Canadian bank near Point Edward, almost opposite Port Huron, Michigan. Nothing is known of her last hours. She sank in Lake Huron, with her entire crew, at a point believed to be about eight miles north of Port Huron.

The steamer *William Nottingham* had left Fort William with a cargo of grain stowed away in her hold, bound for the lower lakes. For many hectic hours she fought her way across Lake Superior until her supply of fuel coal was exhausted. In desperation her crew turned to her cargo of grain for the much needed fuel. Under her boilers and into the fire boxes went the grain and it helped to keep up the steam necessary to keep the ship in motion. Thus handicapped she reached Whitefish Bay. Here she was swept ashore on Sandy Island. Three of her crew perished in a futile attempt to reach help by launching a lifeboat. Several hours later the balance of her crew was rescued by the Coast Guard.

The crew of the *Howard M. Hanna, Jr.,* (former) had a harrowing escape from death in the Big Storm. The *Hanna* cleared Lorain, Ohio, loaded with coal for Milwaukee, where she was to have laid up for the winter —her last trip of the season. She battled the elements until, when off Saginaw Bay, the full fury of the storm struck her. Disabled, she went aground off Port Austin, Michigan. The men aboard suffered greatly from exposure but managed to stay aboard their ship. Slowly she settled into deep water. When her deck was within six inches of being under water, the Coast Guard rescued the half frozen crew. The ship was later refloated and reconditioned and is at present writing still in active lake service under another name.

The big freighter, *Fred G. Hartwell,* steaming through the Big Storm, met difficulty on Gros Cap Reef in Whitefish Bay. When within the comparative safety of the Bay, she was blown on the reef and badly damaged. Her crew were all saved.

The government *Lightship No. 82,* anchored at the entrance to Buffalo harbor, was not to be seen after the Big Storm had subsided. Her entire crew of six men perished. A meager bit of information was afterwards found scrawled on a board from the lightship. It read, "Good bye, Nellie, ship is breaking up fast—Williams." Such were Captain Hugh M. Williams' last words to his wife. The wreck of the little lightship eventually was washed up on the shore.

LORE OF THE LAKES

The Big Storm is said to have had its *"Hesperus"* in the barge *Plymouth*. The U. S. Coast Guards sighted the *Plymouth* in distress on Lake Michigan off St. Martin's Island, and went to her aid. Upon going aboard, death surrounded them. Her crew of seven men were each lashed securely to prevent their being washed or blown overboard. The intense cold had frozen every man to his death. Their ship had outlived the Big Storm, but the crew had not.

Other ships were also victims of the Big Storm to a lesser degree. Some were blown ashore without loss of life and the vessels were later salvaged. Other boats made port safely but were severely damaged.

Such is the tragic story of the Big Storm. The real and complete story of the lost ships, of the terrific human struggle to keep afloat against the devastating elements, will never be known. How the ships and crews battled that early November wind, cold, snow, ice and waves, and lost, is a secret that only the lakes will ever know.

The Big Storm is never to be forgotten in the annals of the Great Lakes.

⚓ ⚓ ⚓ ⚓ ⚓ ⚓ ⚓ ⚓

CHAPTER FOURTEEN

THE STEAMER EASTLAND

In the busy city of Chicago, if one walks to the foot of Randolph Street he may see, moored to the Naval Reserve dock there, the trim ship *U. S. S. Wilmette*. It is now considered one of the finest Naval Reserve training ships in the United States. It has steamed over 150,000 miles and has been perfectly satisfactory in every detail.

As a wreck, she was purchased by the government at a sale, held by the United States Court, early in 1916, to be made into a training vessel. The subsequent remodeling work proceeded slowly, as difficulty was experienced in obtaining materials, for the United States was involved at that time in the World War. It was intended that the ship would be sent to the Atlantic Ocean for war service when completed, but the signing of the Armistice in 1918 cancelled that journey. However, at this time the ship was completed and could have sailed, had it been necessary. Consequently, she never left the Great Lakes. In 1926 further remodeling was done. She was converted to burn oil, and four new watertube boilers were installed. Watertight bulkheads were installed; additional division bulkheads were placed in her bottom, so as to reduce the area of free water; and the pumping system was completely revamped, so that now she conforms to Navy standards in every detail for a vessel of her size.

The *Wilmette* today is a grand ship. But, turn the pages of time back to 1915 when in this same city this ship had the name *Eastland* painted on her high bows.

Its very name still brings a feeling of horror to many a Chicago family, for it was this very ship, that rolled over on its side, while still partially tied to its dock, at seven-twenty on the morning of Saturday, July 24th, 1915. Eight hundred and thirty-five persons, mostly factory workers, their children and their friends, were drowned in the Chicago River near Clark Street!

Thus, to the steamer *Eastland,* goes the ignominious record of the highest number of deaths in one single accident ever to occur on the Great Lakes. Newspapers the world over screamed out news of the terrible disaster in headlines flung across their front pages, and their columns carried long lists of the dead and missing for many days after the catastrophe. The President of the United States, Woodrow Wilson, saddened by the appalling tragedy, ordered a thorough investigation to be made. Secretary William C. Redfield, of the Department of Commerce, hurried to Chicago and conducted the hearings.

Let us look into the history of this ill-fated ship, and see whence she came, and what was her record prior to this accident. We find that she was but twelve years old when this ill luck befell her. This is quite young for a lake passenger ship, many of which operate for forty or more years. She was built at Port Huron, Michigan, in 1903, of steel, and was two hundred and sixty-nine feet in length, and thirty-six feet in beam, and of one thousand nine hundred and sixty-one tons displacement. She had twin propellers, and was said to draw fourteen feet of water.

After her completion at Port Huron, the *Eastland* was sent to Chicago, where she was operated for several seasons in the Lake Michigan excursion trade. She was then sold to a group of Cleveland owners and was brought to that Ohio port about 1908. Here she was acclaimed as "The Speed Queen of the Lakes," and made daily round trips to Cedar Point, Ohio, some sixty miles west along the south shore of Lake Erie. She also made evening "moonlight" lake rides. Excursion boat travel on the lakes was very popular, and many thousands of persons made the trip aboard the *Eastland*. It is reported that in the year 1913 she carried well over two hundred thousand passengers without a single mishap. She was tall and white and very trim, and made an impressive picture as she cut through the waves at her speed of twenty-two miles per hour. On her hurricane deck aft, she carried a steam calliope, upon which was played the popular tunes of the day. Its strains could be heard several miles over the water as the ship sailed her course.

During her operation on the Cleveland to Cedar Point run, she was in the charge of Captain M. S. Thompson, who sailed her for several years without incident. Captain William J. MacLean also served as master of the *Eastland* while on this run. Later Captain C. M. Ennes took her bridge and he sailed her until she was sold, again to Chicago owners, and he delivered the *Eastland* to them in that port.

It is a peculiar fact, that, while she sailed out of Cleveland an insidious rumor arose about the ship, to the effect that she was unsafe for passenger travel. This rumor persisted until it eventually reached the ears of her owners, The Eastland Navigation Company. They endeavored to spike the ill-boding report by inserting in the daily Cleveland newspapers a half page advertisement. It read as follows:

"FIVE THOUSAND DOLLARS REWARD"

"The steamer *Eastland* was built in 1903. She is built of steel and is of ocean type in construction. Her water compartments when filled carry 800 tons of ballast. She is 269 feet long, beam 36 feet, and draws 14 feet of water. She has twin screws driven by two powerful triple expansion engines supplied with steam from four Scotch boilers."

"The material she is built of, the type of her construction, together with the power in her hold, makes her the staunchest, fastest, and safest boat devoted to pleasure on the Great Lakes."

"All this is well known to people acquainted with marine matters. But there are thousands of people who know absolutely nothing about boats, the rules and regulations for their running, and the inspection and licensing of the same by the United States Government. In the hope of influencing this class of people there have been put into circulation, stories to the effect the steamer *Eastland* is not safe."

THE STEAMER EASTLAND

"Unfortunately we do not know who the persons are that have caused to be put into circulation these scandalous stories. Their motives however, are easily guessed. Therefore, in justice to ourselves and in fairness to the 400,000 people that have enjoyed themselves during the past four years in this palatial craft (and that without a single mishap), we offer the above reward to any person that will bring forth a naval engineer, a marine architect, a shipbuilder, or anyone qualified to pass on the merits of a ship, who will say that the steamer *Eastland* is not a seaworthy ship or that she would not ride out any storm or weather any condition that can arise on either lake or ocean."

"THE EASTLAND NAVIGATION COMPANY."

(The above advertisement appeared in The Cleveland Plain Dealer of August 9, 1910.)

In 1914 the Eastland was again a familiar sight on Lake Michigan and again proceeded to make passenger excursions out of Chicago. Her cruises proved popular and were well patronized.

Everything went well with her until the fatal day of her disaster. On this particular day the *Eastland* was to carry, along with the steamer *Theodore Roosevelt* and other boats, an excursion of employees of The Western Electric Company and their friends. Their destination was to have been Michigan City, Indiana. The tickets sold for seventy-five cents, with free transportation for young children. The *Eastland* was then owned by the

Saint Joseph-Chicago Steamship Company, and was leased to the Indiana Transportation Company.

She was in charge of Captain Harry Pedersen and Chief Engineer J. M. Ericson. They both survived the disaster. The luckless captain was at his post standing on the proud ship's bridge, as the huge crowd of picnic passengers in gala summer attire jammed the decks and cabins of the ship. Estimates were that about twenty-five hundred persons were aboard. The band played gaily. The gang-plank was hauled away. A tug was at the *Eastland's* bow. The stern line was slacked off. Passengers began to notice the extraordinary slant of the ship's decks. No one was unduly alarmed until the list increased. Loose chairs and unattached furniture began to slide to the port side. In the refreshment stand the refrigerator tore loose and toppled over. Finally passengers themselves could no longer hold their positions on the ship and all were slid in a struggling mass against the port rail and the inner cabin walls. The ship continued to list and, in what observers variously estimated to be from five to fifteen minutes, the *Eastland* toppled completely over on her port side in twenty-one feet of water. Her starboard side lay flat, about fifteen feet above the surface of the water. Mad bedlam prevailed. Hundreds of persons were thrown into the river, some fortunately caught boxes, crates, furniture and wreckage, and swam to safety. Those caught inside the cabins were drowned with little chance to get free. Still others, unable to swim, went down in the struggling, fighting mass of floating humanity.

Many days were required to locate the dead. Many

bodies were removed through holes cut by acetylene torches into the side of the ship that still lay above the water. A few were not found until the ship had been righted and floated.

The grim stroke of sudden death and disaster was over. Wreckers took over the formidable task of removing the wrecked hulk from the river. The open holes in her sides were patched and the *Eastland* was righted and floated again. She never since has been in the passenger trade, and it is most unlikely that she ever will. She appears to have found a useful pursuit in the nature of a well kept training ship.

Many and complicated were the lawsuits that followed the *Eastland* disaster, and many were the hours spent by boards of inquiry faithfully endeavoring to arrive at its actual cause. Practically all of the ship's licensed officers, and many of the crew, were placed under arrest and ordered to appear at various inquests and investigations.

The public, appalled at the tragedy, but being unfamiliar with the matters of the construction and handling of a ship, at first was inclined to blame the captain; then the engineer; then the alleged overcrowding; then the possible rush of the passengers to the ship's side. The rumored unseaworthiness of the vessel was again brought forth and considered.

Official investigators had a serious problem, with great responsibilities. Resulting directly from their findings has come safer Great Lakes and ocean passenger travel. Now all passenger vessels are more carefully inspected and licensed to carry only such numbers of passengers as is absolutely safe.

Water ballast tanks are constantly watched and checked. Life boat, raft, and belt equipment is rigidly and regularly inspected, and provisions are made for equipment to accommodate all the passengers that a ship is licensed to carry. The United States does not want its citizens' lives placed in jeopardy when they travel the water. Responsible officials learn through such terrible examples as the *Eastland* catastrophe how water travel can be further protected and life made safer and more comfortable.

More than twenty years after the *Eastland* disaster, on August 7th, 1935, there appeared in the Cleveland Plain Dealer, what is probably the last mention of the appalling affair that will be found among the news items concerning the disaster. It read:

"EASTLAND CASE BOBS UP"
"U. S. Appeals Court Upholds Decision in 1915 Steamer Disaster"

"Chicago, Aug. 7.—(AP)—The United States Circuit Court of Appeals today upheld a District Court ruling that the St. Joseph-Chicago Steamship Co., former owners of the steamer *Eastland,* which sank in the Chicago River July 24, 1915, is not liable for the 835 deaths in the disaster."

"The court held that the company was liable only to the extent of the salvage value of the vessel; that the boat was seaworthy; that the operators had taken proper precautions and that the responsibility was traced to an engineer who neglected to fill the ballast tanks properly."

⚓ ⚓ ⚓ ⚓ ⚓ ⚓ ⚓ ⚓

Chapter Fifteen

BLACK FRIDAY

The whaleback freighter, *James B. Colgate,* lay at her dock in Buffalo. The new mate of the steamer turned to a fresh page in the ship's log book and headed it "Friday, October 20, 1916." It was just after midnight and the finishing touches of loading a cargo of hard coal had just been completed. The ship was ready to sail on a voyage to the Canadian head of the lakes, Fort William, Ontario.

Little did the mate realize that the date he had just written was one never to be forgotten in the annals of lake shipping, and henceforth would be known by the mariners as "Black Friday." Many other things the mate did not realize, as he headed the clean page. This was to be his last voyage. He was doomed never to arrive at his destination. Moreover, the same terrible fate was to be meted out to the entire crew, save one man alone, the captain, two weeks in command. The ship was never to be seen again. Little of all this the mate understood.

Captain Walter J. Grashaw had sailed the lakes for nearly twenty years, ten of which were spent as mate aboard the *Colgate.* Two weeks previously he had been given command of the ship. A seasoned sailorman he was. He noted the rising wind and could hear the tumbling waves beat themselves against the near by breakwall as, at one-ten on that eventful morning, he sailed his ship

from the protecting harbor of Buffalo out into the inky
blackness of Lake Erie. Strong winds were nothing new
to Captain Grashaw. He had weathered many. His ship,
he knew, had also weathered many. Built at Superior,
Wisconsin, in 1892, she had therefore, twenty-four years
sailing experience to her credit. She had met many a blow
in those active years and had always come through on
top. But this was Black Friday, and it was going to be
different from any other blow she had ever encountered.

The *Colgate* made slow headway in that roaring gale
and dawn found her just nearing Long Point on the
Canadian shore. She battle fiercely with the howling
hurricane all that day. Lake Erie, the shallowest of the
five Great Lakes, and consequently more easily riled,
beat giant combers over the *Colgate's* decks and tossed her
about like a chip.

Captain and crew struggled to keep the ship headed
into the wind. No one slept. By nightfall the foaming
seas were a fury to behold. They crashed themselves
against the shuddering vessel and beat upon her hatch
coverings. Gradually, she began to take water in her hold.
It sloshed around with her cargo and stayed there. Pumps
worked furiously, but they were no match for the tumbling tons of water that banged themselves upon the ship.

At eight o'clock that night the *Colgate* began to list.
It was then that the crew abandoned hope for their ship.
They fell upon their knees and prayed. They talked of
their families, their wives and children, their mothers and
fathers, and their sweethearts. A man facing death
always thinks of his loved ones, if he is spared the time

in which to think. They prayed that they might yet be saved.

The list grew worse. It commenced to rain, but that mattered little to their already sorry plight. It only made the night that much blacker. Captain Grashaw, in oil-skins, went out on his heaving bridge, risking being blown bodily into the maelstrom, and lighted the ship's search-light. It pierced the night with an eerie beam. The skipper hoped that it might attract another and more fortunate ship to their assistance; but there was no other ship. The *Colgate* carried no radio; and the ship-to-shore telephone was yet to come. The captain turned the rays of the searchlight down on the broad deck of his ship. He could see the hatch covers strain and raise at their fast-eners, from the immense pressure of the tumbling water and cargo within the hold. He realized that his ship could not last much longer. He knew that no vessel could stand such a beating and still hold together.

Her bow was now low in the water and it went slowly deeper and deeper. At ten that night the ship slid quietly downward, bow first, to the bottom of Lake Erie. No wreckage floated. Anything not firmly attached to the ship had long since been torn loose and washed overboard. There was nothing to which the struggling crew in the water might cling. They had life preservers about them, which helped keep them afloat for a short while, but the icy waves crashed over the doomed men and drowned them.

Numbed by the stinging cold and the tragedy, Captain Grashaw found himself in the surging water. Destiny pushed a life raft toward him. It bumped him as he struggled in the water. It was the only bit of floating wreckage in those turbulent waters; just a small raft, no larger than five by nine feet. Somehow it had miraculously drifted from the sinking *Colgate*. Two men were already on it and they helped their captain climb aboard. Their eyes had by now become accustomed to the darkness and they could distinguish objects about them.

The three men clung to the raft; one a coal passer; another an engineer; and the captain. High seas dashed the tiny craft about perilously and finally succeeded in rolling it completely over and tossing the miserable men on it back into the water. The coal passer was never seen again. The captain clung on and managed to pull the engineer back on with him. The devilish night at last gave way to daylight.

As the dawn came, the raft again flipped over and once more the two men clawed back on it, but the engineer was exhausted. Captain Grashaw saw him slipping slowly into the water. He struggled to keep him aboard the tossing raft but to no avail. The weakened engineer slipped silently beneath the waves. Now the captain was alone. Twenty-six men about him had all perished, his entire crew. Many times he almost gave up, but somehow courage and the strength to hang on would return. He beat his arms, legs and body against the raft to keep circulation in them. The waves lessened a bit and the hanging onto the raft became easier. All that Saturday he clung to the raft and, as darkness settled upon the subsiding waters, he wondered if he would ever again see daylight.

BLACK FRIDAY

That night the passenger steamer from Buffalo to Detroit passed nearby. He shouted and waved his arms, but no one aboard the passing ship heard nor saw him and it soon disappeared, leaving him to his fate.

Sunday morning dawned, and with it fortune favored the now almost dead ship master. A deep whistle from behind him sounded over the waters and he turned to see the most welcome sight he had ever beheld. The carferry *Marquette & Bessemer No. 2* was steaming to his aid. The officers in her pilot house had spotted the helpless raft with its lone survivor. Her skipper, Captain Van Buskirk, ordered the carferry stopped and willing hands helped Captain Grashaw aboard. Almost dead from exposure and hunger and dazed by his terrible experiences, he was at first unable to tell of the tragedy. Given food and dry, warm blankets and put to bed, he was taken to Conneaut, Ohio, and thence to a hospital, where he eventually recovered.

Mrs. Grashaw hastened to her husband's bedside and great was her relief to find him alive.

To Captain Walter J. Grashaw had come a harrowing experience that fortunately few sailormen are called upon to undergo, but constantly must face in their chosen life work. His story of courage and grit pales fiction. He passed away twelve years after his thrilling experience with angry Lake Erie.

More fortunate was the crew of thirteen men of the steamer *Marshall F. Butters,* a wooden lumber carrier, caught in the same storm-swept Lake Erie on the same

213

day, Black Friday. The *Butters* was bound for Cleveland with a cargo of shingles and lumber. She had left the mouth of the Detroit River and was headed for the Southeast Shoals Light.

The wind grew stronger and the waves higher. The *Butters* began to roll heavily in the rising seas and her cargo began to shift, causing the ship to list. Captain McClure of the *Butters* ordered his men to trim the cargo, hoping to right the ship, but the old lumber hooker was doomed. The crew, composed mostly of men from around Ludington, Michigan, worked frantically to save their vessel, but the inrushing water was too much for them.

Captain McClure sounded the distress signal on the ship's whistle, but it could hardly be heard above the shrieking of the wind. Soon the ship settled lower in the water and the fires in her boilers were extinguished. She drifted now at the mercy of the wind and the waves. Ten of the crew took to the lifeboats while the captain and two men remained aboard the sinking ship.

The plight of the *Butters* was sighted by the large freighters, the *Frank R. Billings* of the Pioneer Steamship Company and the *F. G. Hartwell*. Captain F. B. Cody of the *Billings* noticed the puffs of white steam come from the doomed ship's whistle, although he was unable to hear the sound. In spite of the high seas he circled the *Billings* about and, with the aid of storm oil spread upon the water, he managed to get close enough to get a line aboard the *Butters*. His crew pulled the three men to safety aboard the *Billings,* and brought them to Cleveland. The ten men that took off in the lifeboat were rescued by the steamer *Hartwell* and taken to Fairport. The *Butters* sank beneath the waves of Lake Erie at a point twelve miles from the Southeast Shoals.

"Worst storm I ever experienced," said the rescued Captain McClure, "I regret that the ship and cargo were lost, but thank Heaven every man in the crew was saved. That wind blew seventy miles an hour."

Another skipper to lose his ship and crew in the gale of Black Friday was Captain John Mattison. He alone was saved. His ship was the wooden schooner *D. L. Filer*. She had a cargo of coal from Buffalo bound for Saugatuck, Michigan. One of the last of the sailing fleet on the Great Lakes, the *Filer* had some forty-five years of service to her credit. She carried a crew of seven men, mostly Norwegian. She was a small ship, being only three hundred and fifty-seven tons burden.

For two days after leaving Buffalo the *Filer* had tough going. The high seas beat the old ship unmercifully. Near Bar Point at the mouth of the Detroit River and within sight of comparative safety, the wooden hull of the little vessel began to ship water. Her seams opened and she soon become unmanageable. The water came in the hold faster than the men could pump it out and she slowly settled to the bottom of the lake in eighteen feet of water.

Her crew climbed the foremast which still protruded above the water. Six men clung to that mast. Their

215

weight proved too much for the old mast and it cracked off, throwing the men into the water. Five of them perished. The sixth swam to the aftermast to which Captain Mattison had climbed alone, and the two men clung all night to this mast.

During the night a large steamer passed within sight of the men and they shouted themselves hoarse in a futile effort to attract the attention of the steamer, but she sailed on, not hearing their calls. Dawn brought the Detroit & Cleveland passenger steamer *Western States* with Captain Salem Robinson in command. The two survivors were sighted by the steamer and a boat was put out to take off the two men on the mast. While the rescue boat made its way toward the two men, one of them was seen to lose his grasp on the mast and to sink beneath the waves. He perished. Captain Mattison along clung fast and was taken off. Aboard the steamer he was made comfortable and lived to tell his gruesome tale—another captain minus his ship and crew.

Still another ship perished in that frightful gale of Black Friday. But this one left only floating bodies of its captain and crew to mutely tell of the horrors of those last hours of fighting the wind and waves.

She was the Canadian steamer *Merida* with twenty-three men aboard. All were lost. No word of what occurred will ever be told of the sinking of the *Merida*.

BLACK FRIDAY

Days later bodies of her crew were found floating in mid-lake with life preservers on bearing the name of the *Merida*. She had been sighted by Captain J. F. Massey of the steamer *Briton,* in Lake Erie. The *Merida* was having tough going and the waves were beating the ship badly when Captain Massey sighted her. The *Briton* also was taking a terrible beating, and only a miracle brought her in the shelter of Cedar Point. It is believed that the *Merida* went down about ten miles southeast of the Southeast Shoals.

For many days after the lake subsided, the revenue cutter *Morrill* searched Lake Erie for the bodies of the men that were aboard these ill-fated ships, and many were found. Passing ships also located many. They were taken ashore and were subsequently identified by relatives.

Sailormen of the Great Lakes will always talk of Black Friday on Lake Erie. The day is written indelibly in their minds and they will pass it on to the new-comers with the sage advice, "Sailor, Beware."

Chapter Sixteen

THE FREIGHTER

Nowhere afloat are there fleets of freight steamers like those on the Great Lakes. The modern lake freighter is the result of many years development. Men like John Fitch, Robert Fulton, James Watt, John Ericsson, Thomas Edison and hundreds of others have all contributed something toward the building of the highly efficient lake vessel of today.

Nowhere afloat are ships that transport such immense volumes of bulk freight so economically and efficiently. The modern freight steamer compares with the modern factory ashore. Factories turn out a product, whereas the product of the lake freighter is *transported tonnage*. It is operated as carefully and intelligently as any well regulated manufacturing plant on land. The one thought uppermost in the minds of all concerned in the operation of the freighter is to efficiently and economically turn out *transported tonnage*, with safety to life and property ever in mind.

The tonnage so transported is largely bulk freight, although there are also floated on the lakes great quantities of what the lake men call "package freight," meaning purely commercial freight, of almost any size and shape. The bulk freight consists mainly of iron ore, followed by coal, grain, crushed stone, cement, slag, chemicals and sand. Specially designed tankers transport vast amounts of gasoline and various oil products. In fact, so highly efficient have the lake fleets become, that there is a type of ship built to handle almost every major commodity with the utmost dispatch.

Most of the vessels are loaded and unloaded by equipment on the dock, but there is an ever growing fleet of "self-unloaders." These ships are so constructed that they can unload their cargo onto a dock with no assistance whatever from the shore. The portland cement carriers unload their cement by chuting it with air pressure from the ship into the plant on the dock. The lake tanker is no different from its salt water sister, in that it can load its own cargo and also discharge it at destination.

A unique type of ship has been developed especially for transporting cargo between the eastern seaports and the lake ports via the Hudson River and the New York State Canal. Because of canal conditions these ships must be constructed differently than other ships. Consequently, the "canaler" type of vessel is now a familiar sight in most all ports on the lakes and along the Atlantic coast. These sturdy ships of shallow draft, squatting low in the water, with stubby stack and low deck houses, navigate both the lakes and the ocean with equal ease. They are Diesel powered. One of these vessels frequently makes trips between a Texas port and the Great Lakes.

Sand boats suck their cargoes of building sands from the bottom of the lakes and unload themselves at their destination. Package freighters, while not self loading, are so designed that a minimum of manual labor is required. Specially constructed freighters carry automobiles between lake ports.

Carferries transport whole trains across the lakes. Two such ships of the Pere Marquette Railroad fleet, are recently reported, within the past ten years of operation on Lake Michigan, as having covered more miles, moved more freight per mile, and given steady employment to more persons than any two ships afloat. They traveled 1,986,660 miles, or the equivalent of eight times around the earth at the equator. They served 1,614,200 crew meals while the ships operated every day, winter and summer. Almost $2,000,000 was paid as wages to officers and crews. There were no fatal accidents.

Scrap iron carriers can unload with their own magnetized cranes. The press of modern business has forced ship owners to keep their ships apace with the times.

The globe-trotting salt water tramp is finding its way into the Great Lakes, more and more. During the past few years it is almost a daily sight to view one of these ships loading or discharging cargo to or from a foreign port. Buffalo, Cleveland, Detroit and Chicago are the principal United States ports of call for the foreign owned boats. During the winter months, when the lakes are frozen over and navigation impossible, these ships ply their trade on salt water.

A recent issue of the United States Steel News describes "the typical bulk freighter as about six hundred feet long, sixty to sixty-five feet wide and has a molded depth of thirty-two feet. The pilot house occupies the extreme fore end of the ship and the propelling machinery the extreme aft end, leaving the intervening space for the accommodation of cargo. The cargo section of the vessel is covered by hatches, spaced either at twelve or twenty-four foot centers, and extending nearly across the full width of the ship. When loading or unloading the vessel the hatch covers are removed, thereby throwing the deck almost completely open. A ship of this type can carry eleven to fourteen thousand gross tons of iron ore on a twenty foot draft, but is built to draw twenty-two feet when that depth of water is available. An increase of two feet in draft increases the carrying capacity fifteen hundred to two thousand tons."

The shipping season on the Great Lakes is limited to approximately seven and one-half months. Masters often force their ships through ice packs at the start of the season and again at the close. Occasionally in the late fall, a ship will be stuck fast in the ice, particularly in the narrow and shallow channels of the northern rivers, and be forced to stay there until the following spring. Crews so marooned tell of deer and moose walking out to the ships over the ice and eating food tossed overboard to them.

A record, still standing, for the fastest loading of an ore boat cargo occurred on September 7, 1921, at Two Harbors, Minnesota. The steamer loaded was the *D. G. Kerr* of the Pittsburgh Steamship fleet. At that time she was under the command of Captain W. P. McElroy of Cleveland. Through the efficient co-operation of Mr. George Watts, the dock superintendent, and all employees concerned, this almost unbelievable loading was made. In the extremely short space of sixteen and one-half minutes there were dumped into the hold of the six-hundred foot ship exactly twelve thousand five hundred and seven tons of iron ore. This is at the astonishing rate of seven hundred and fifty-eight tons of ore per minute! The vessel's time alongside the dock—from arrival to clearing—was nineteen minutes! However, the average loading time of the ships is about three hours and forty-two minutes, which is also a record to be proud of.

Unloading a ship of bulk freight requires more time than loading, as the material must be scooped from the ship's hold and carried to the dock and there dumped. A record for unloading iron ore goes to the steamer *Henry H. Rogers,* also of the Pittsburgh Steamship Company fleet. This ship was relieved of twelve thousand and nine tons of the red ore in exactly two hours and twenty-five minutes, at Conneaut, Ohio, on June 15, 1929. The average time consumed for unloading a modern vessel with twelve thousand five hundred gross tons of ore is about three hours and thirty minutes.

These are achievements almost unbelievable to the salt water navigator, who considers himself fast if he gets his hatch covers off in the time it required the *D. G. Kerr* to load her entire cargo.

A great amount of the iron ore floated down the Great Lakes comes from the enormous deposits known as the Mesabi Range. This range lies in what is called the Minnesota Arrowhead. Untold millions of dollars in ore have, and will be taken from the Mesabi.

THE FREIGHTER

How this section became a part of the United States is interesting, and the consequent results are stupendous. Historians differ in giving the credit to the individual actually responsible.

One story has it that, back in England in 1755, one Dr. John Mitchell, who is said to have been a London physician, drew a map of the British Colonies in North America. This map was used to establish the International Boundary. At the head of the Great Lakes he followed, as boundary, the Pigeon River while he might as well have used the St. Louis River out of Duluth. Thus, the slip of his pen threw the great ore fields into the United States.

The other story tells of Benjamin Franklin, in a canny mood, while establishing the boundary line of the new United States at this point, chose the northernmost of two rivers that flowed into the head of the Great Lakes, and then spread fan shape into the wilderness. The section of the fan contained the Mesabi and other great iron ore ranges and thus became United States territory.

Many years later the ore deposits were discovered, and subsequently developed into what is now the largest and greatest of the world's producing iron districts. This, in a large measure, accounts for the vast lake traffic of today.

The modern lake freighters of today, such as the *John Hulst, Governor Miller, Harry Coulby, Carl D. Bradley* and *L. E. Block,* have been evolved from all the types of freighters that have sailed the lakes before them. Such ships as the *Walk-in-the-Water* of 1818; *Vandalia* of 1841; *Merchant* of 1861; *Onoko* of 1882; *Superior City*

223

of 1898; *Augustus B. Wolvin* of 1904 and many others, all have contributed their part.

Each ship, as it was built, incorporated the successful experiments of its predecessors, and itself contained new experiments. Many, many of these experiments were sooner or later discarded as impractical, but those that stood the test of time were continued. Wrecks were studied to locate weak points in construction. As ships were built longer and deeper they had to be duly strengthened and braced. Some vessels actually broke in two shortly after they were built because men had not yet learned how to construct them. The steam engine was constantly being improved. Today the foresight of man continues to improve his ships and their engines. Improvement and advancement never stop.

Looking back at the steamers mentioned as outstanding types of improvement, one comes first to the *Walk-in-the-Water*. This little vessel, the first to carry steam on the lakes, is described in detail elsewhere in this book.

The first screw propeller to appear on the lakes was in 1841, the *Vandalia*, a tiny ship when compared with ships of today. She was but one hundred and thirty-eight tons, ninety-one feet on deck, twenty feet two inches in beam and eight feet three inches in depth and of wood construction. She carried sails, sloop rigged. She had a small cabin on deck for passengers. Captain John Ericsson had shortly before invented the screw propeller and into the *Vandalia* went the new underwater contrivance. Built in the winter of 1840-41 at Oswego, New York, she operated several years, mostly on Lake Ontario, and was then enlarged to three hundred and twenty tons. Her name was then changed to *Milwaukee*.

Previous steamers were all of the sidewheel type with their engines placed amidships. In the *Vandalia* the engine was placed near the stern and below deck. This was to be later adopted as the standard for all lake freighters. The *Vandalia* proved a success and soon other vessels of her type appeared on the waters of the lakes.

The next radical departure from the usual, was the package freight steamer *Merchant,* built in 1861. She has the distinction of being the first commercial vessel to be built of iron on the lakes. Ever expanding in size, the *Merchant* was six hundred and fifty tons and was one hundred and ninety feet in length, twenty-nine feet beam and fourteen feet depth. She is reported to have cost sixty thousand dollars. The *Merchant* operated successfully until about 1878 when she was lost in a storm. Her engines were salvaged and placed in another ship. Her success proved to the vesselmen of those days that iron was a practical material for their ships. The *Merchant,* built by J. C. Evans and his son, E. T. Evans, of Buffalo, was the forerunner of the present day Great Lakes Transit Company fleet.

Time marched on. About 1880 the ore trade was becoming a bigger factor in lake shipping tonnage. Boats were being built to carry the red mineral exclusively. The ore boat of today was then being born. So it was in 1882 that the *Onoko,* the first ore carrier to be built of iron, was launched in the yards of the Globe Iron Works in Cleveland. Builders, still expanding their ships, made the

Onoko three hundred and two and one-half feet long, over all, thirty-nine feet beam, and twenty-five feet depth, with a capacity of three thousand tons. She was the true prototype of the modern freighter. The *Onoko* spurred the demand for better and faster dock loading and unloading equipment. Efficiency was coming to the lakes in great strides.

The *Onoko* was also an outstanding success. She was at first rigged with sails to aid her engine in making better speed and to reduce operating costs. Sails were subsequently abandoned and steam was depended upon exclusively. The *Onoko* operated successfully over a period of thirty-three years, coming to her end in a storm on Lake Superior in 1915. Before the *Onoko* left the active list, ships twice her length and triple her capacity had been launched. Ore carrying rates had been reduced by the increasing efficiency so that they were almost one-half of what they had been when the ship was built.

Probably the steamer *Superior City,* launched April 13, 1898, in the yards of what is now the American Shipbuilding Company at Lorain, Ohio, is the best illustration of the next step in the advancement of the lake freighter. When launched, the *Superior City* was the largest vessel ever built on freshwater. Lorain declared a holiday as the whole town crowded the river front to watch the monster vessel slide down the ways. She was four hundred and thirty feet keel, fifty feet beam and twenty-eight feet six inches in depth. Her gross tonnage was four thousand seven hundred and ninety-five tons and her capacity was seven thousand one hundred tons.

THE FREIGHTER

The *Superior City* sailed the lakes for twenty-two years and came to an untimely end in a collision with the steamer *Willis L. King* in Whitefish Bay, Lake Superior, on August 20, 1920. The accident occurred about nine-thirty in the evening, as the *Superior City* was down-bound with some seven thousand tons of iron ore in her hold. The *Willis L. King* was upound, without cargo. A large hole was torn in the port side, aft of amidships, and, as the ship settled, an explosion blew the departing crew into the water. The *Superior City* sank instantly in deep water. Four men of her crew were rescued. Twenty-eight men and one woman drowned. No bodies were recovered. The ship had, however, served her purpose as a stepping-stone to better vessels on the lakes.

Improvements after the *Superior City* came rapidly. The *Augustus B. Wolvin,* which was launched in 1904, is five hundred and sixty feet long, fifty-six feet beam and thirty-two feet depth. At the time of launching she was acclaimed as the largest freshwater ship afloat. Other steamers followed the *Wolvin* into the water in the succeeding years, each one an improvement over the former.

On April 30, 1927, the steamer *Harry Coulby* slipped into the water from the ways at the American Shipbuilding Company's plant at Lorain, Ohio. The *Coulby* is outstanding in lake freight vessels. Her length over all is six hundred and thirty feet, nine inches, molded breadth sixty-five feet, molded depth thirty-three feet, and fourteen thousand tons capacity. The vessel was built to the highest class in Lloyd's and the American Bureau of Shipping for lake service. Crew accommodations are of the

227

best. She has elaborate quarters for a limited number of guests.

On her maiden trip from Lorain to the head of the lakes she transported fourteen thousand, six hundred and fifty tons of coal. On her return trip down the lakes she carried thirteen thousand seven hundred and thirty-one tons of iron ore. The *Harry Coulby* is the flagship of the Interlake Steamship Company's fleet and is operated by Pickands, Mather & Company of Cleveland.

The latest additions to the lakes' fleet of bulk freight ships are the *William A. Irvin,* the *Governor Miller,* the *Ralph H. Watson* and the *John Hulst.* The first two mentioned were built at the yards of the American Shipbuilding Company at Lorain and the latter two at the Great Lakes Engineering Works at River Rouge, Detroit. All four ships were built for the Pittsburgh Steamship Company, a United States Steel Corporation subsidiary, and are practically duplicates, varying only in minor details.

The four new vessels were all launched during the winter of 1937-38. Statistics' prophecy is that these four great ships can look forward to an overage of forty years of active service on the Great Lakes. Man wonders what the modern lake ships will look like when these four vessels are relegated to the discard as obsolete. Will they be larger, faster and more streamlined, or have they now reached their zenith?

Many other modern ships have been built for other lines of trade on the Great Lakes. Outstanding in the oil

THE FREIGHTER

industry is the *Red Crown,* largest tanker at present on freshwater. She was built for the Standard Oil Company of Indiana by the Manitowoc Shipbuilding Company in 1937, and has a keel length of four hundred and thirty-four feet, beam of fifty-five feet and depth of twenty-eight feet.

To the steamer *Carl D. Bradley* of the Bradley Transportation Company, a United States Steel Corporation subsidiary, with headquarters at Rogers City, Michigan, goes the record of being the longest overall length ship on the Great Lakes. Her dimensions are six hundred and thirty-eight feet nine inches overall length, sixty-five feet beam and thirty-three feet depth. The gross tonnage of the *Carl D. Bradley* is ten thousand and twenty-eight tons. She was built in 1927 and is of the self-unloading type. With this equipment the *Bradley* can unload her entire cargo onto a dock with no assistance from shore facilities. Crushed stone is the usual cargo of the big vessel.

Another record also is held by the *Carl D. Bradley.* She carried the largest single cargo ever transported on the Great Lakes. During the summer of 1929 she loaded eighteen thousand one hundred and fourteen tons of limestone at Calcite, Michigan, for Gary, Indiana. Estimating this at sixty tons of the crushed stone per railroad car, it would require more than three hundred cars to move the huge cargo on land, which would make up into three of the longest freight trains ordinarily moved today. A truly remarkable water transportation record!

From the largest fleet of ships on the Great Lakes, that

of the Canada Steamship Lines, comes the freighter *Lemoyne* to claim the second highest honors in the matter of overall length and a record cargo also. The *Lemoyne* is six hundred and thirty-three feet in overall length, seventy feet beam and thirty-three feet in depth. She was built in 1926. When it comes to hauling grain, all ships salute the *Lemoyne*. In the summer of 1929 she carried seventeen thousand one hundred and seventy-three net tons of wheat in a single cargo, which amounts to the amazing figure of 571,885 bushels.

It might be mentioned that both these record cargoes referred to above, were, of course, carried under extremely favorable conditions. As a general thing, the capacity of these vessels would be somewhat less than the tonnages indicated above. Also, since 1937, load line requirements promulgated by the government have had the effect of limiting loading depths in some instances.

Almost every season finds some sort of new record established on the Great Lakes; some stand for years while others last but a short while. The largest single cargo carried, in any commodity, is always an interesting item for the lake enthusiasts. Just when it appears that a peak is reached, along comes a ship, sometimes the same one, with just a few more tons of cargo in her hold, and up goes a new record. Such record breaking cargoes are, of course, dependent upon the depth of water in the shallowest channels through which the ship must pass. Water levels on the lakes vary from year to year, even changing slightly from month to month, and record cargoes can be hung up only during those years that nature favors the skipper by giving him deep enough water in which to sail his heavily laden ship.

The present record-breaking single cargo of iron ore ever carried, came down the lakes from Ashland, Wisconsin, in July, 1940, when the steamer *Harry Coulby* broke her own previous record and brought fifteen thousand nine hundred and eight gross tons into a south Lake Michigan port. It is reported that it required two hundred and ninety-eight railroad ore cars to haul the big cargo to the dock from the mines and that it was loaded into the ship from 8:35 A. M. to 3 that same afternoon. The steamer *L. E. Block* is a formidable contender for the honor of carrying the largest iron ore cargo, having hauled several record cargoes in the recent past.

These days records of all kinds usually fall quickly. The largest ship is soon outclassed. The largest cargo is soon exceeded. On and on goes the struggle to do better. It is to be hoped that this urge to improve may never cease.

It is stated by competent authorities that the Great Lakes' commerce is 36.8% of the total United States normal domestic commerce in volume and 16% of normal value. Almost two-thirds of the commercial vessels on the lakes are of United States registry and the tonnage percentage is even higher, it is reported. On May 1, 1939, there were said to be four hundred and sixty-four freighters and sixty-two passenger vessels of over one hundred gross tons under the American flag, compared with two hundred and forty-one freighters and nineteen passenger ships of Canadian registry.

231

LORE OF THE LAKES

Of growing importance is the outlet from the Great Lakes at Chicago, where barges can be brought from the Mississippi River ports via the system of canals and rivers connecting the two points. Recently, Chicago river folk saw for the first time the odd sight of the ornate old Mississippi River tow boat, with its large stern paddle wheel, moving with its barges along the Chicago harbor. The immense importance of the water transportation system afforded by the Great Lakes, its tributaries and connections is still not fully appreciated by the average citizen.

It is not uncommon for private pleasure craft to make the cruise "from Chicago to Chicago" by going down the drainage canal to the Mississippi River; across the Gulf of Mexico; around or across Florida; thence up the Eastern Coast via the Intracoastal Waterway—a series of canals and rivers which eliminates the necessity of going out into the ocean—to the Hudson River; thence through the Erie or New York State Barge Canal from Albany to Buffalo; and then, via the lakes, back to Chicago.

Here or there in some remote spot along the shores of the Great Lakes, may rest the rotting remains of an old wooden lumber "hooker." None of them now plies the lakes in this trade as they did in the nineties. This romantic angle of lake shipping has gone. The northern forests about the lakes have given their all to the woodsmen's axe.

On a hot day in July, 1935, the author witnessed the final trip of what was probably the last of the old wooden lumber carriers. It was the creaking old "hooker," *I. Wat-*

THE FREIGHTER

son Stephenson, which, stern first, was being towed from her dock, down the Cuyahoga River in Cleveland by two small puffing tugs to the lake front. Here she was to be sunk and used as a breakwater shelter for small craft. The *Stephenson* looked strangely like a ghost ship as she came slowly along; no smoke curled from her stack; a ship out of yesterday, her high wooden sides bare of paint, showing plainly the ugly scars of many victorious battles of bygone years with wind and ice.

Arriving at her last destination, she was swung into exact position by long cables attached to a truck crane on the shore. Conversation with the gray-haired crane operator brought out some interesting facts about the old ship. He had once been her chief engineer.

"She was a splendid boat in those days," he remarked, "one of the finest in the lumber business and I was a proud young fellow to be her engineer. Never thought then that I would be officiating at an affair like this. Sort of a funeral!"

Looking sadly at the old ship, he continued, "Her owner had a suite of rooms built into her that would rival any passenger ship parlors of today. All finished in cherry. He used to make a trip or two every season with us and, when he wasn't aboard, he had it filled with his friends. She sure was a grand old ship!" he mused again.

Then they opened her rusty seacocks and she slowly settled on the bottom of Lake Erie with just enough of her hull showing to bring out her fine lines. At present writing she is still there.

The *I. Watson Stephenson,* typical lumber "hooker," was a steamer that had successfully navigated the lakes for forty years. She was one hundred and seventy-two feet keel and thirty-five feet beam and was built in 1895 at the plant of the F. W. Wheeler Shipbuilding Company at Bay City, Michigan. She was purchased by a former lumber man, Mr. I. Watson Stephenson, named after him, and put into the trade that brought lumber down from the northern lakes to Cleveland and other lower lake ports. During intervals when the lumber business was slack, she carried pulp-wood, paper and sometimes coal.

She later was bought by the Saginaw Bay Transportation Company, and finally passed into the possession of William B. Boom of Cleveland. He eventually removed her machinery and disposed of her hull as mentioned. Thus ended a highly satisfactory career of a type of lake ship that never again will be seen hauling loads of fresh smelling north woods lumber piled high on her deck, into the docks of the lower lakes.

Another, but much later type of lake ship which is passing, is the waleback, or what the men of the lakes call "pig." There are still a few of these ships plying the lakes at present, but none have been constructed for many years and, quite likely, never will.

The whaleback was built for bulk cargo. These vessels had long low rounded sides which brought their deck close to the surface of the water when the ship was loaded. Sailors said that they looked like a giant cigar floating in the water. One passenger ship of this type was built, the steamer *Christopher Columbus,* but all the others were bulk carriers. All were of steel construction.

THE FREIGHTER

All the whalebacks were built by Alexander McDougall and his associates in the nineties, at Duluth, and for many years were familiar sights on the Great Lakes. Today they are rare. Some were dismantled, such as the *J. T. Reid*, formerly the *Washburn*, after a successful career of many years; some were lost on the lakes, as was the *Clifton*, formerly the *Samuel Mather*, with all hands, on Lake Huron in 1924; others, like the *South Park*, formerly the *Frank Rockefeller*, are still on the active list.

An interesting sight along the Detroit and St. Clair Rivers about 1880, was the powerful tugs of that day towing long lines of sailing ships astern. Popular among such tugs were the *Champion*, the *Samson* and the *Sweepstakes*. Often, five or more schooners in a single tow were piloted through the rivers between Lake Erie and Lake Huron. When safely out in open water the tow lines were cast off, the schooners hoisted sail and continued on their way up or down the lakes.

In those days busy wooden shipbuilding yards dotted the lake shores. Ports now almost forgotten were thriving. Masters often owned all or a part of the sailing vessel they commanded, and transacted the ship's business from her deck.

Such a skipper was Captain Oscar B. Smith, of the busy port of Huron, Ohio. Here, on the Huron River, was located the big shipbuilding yard of Valentine Fries. Captain Smith was of the days of "wooden ships and iron men." He sailed the lakes for many years, commanding and owning such schooners as the *La Petite*, *C. K. Clint* and others. Gruff, but kindly underneath, he was a

235

respected man wherever he went. He would always remark to his wife at the finish of each cruise, "Well, Hettie, I brought the ship back with me again." This he always did. After an active and successful career he retired and lived to a ripe old age.

The lakes were larger and more treacherous to those men, and their ships were not as dependable. Wind sent them along, sometimes too strenuously and sometimes not at all. Nevertheless, these men sailed out on the lakes and laid the foundation for the vast lake traffic floated today.

Skippers of those days are now becoming scarce, and their exciting stories of the "iron men and wooden boats" are all but forgotten. One such typical skipper is Captain William P. Benham, who is, at present, retired and living in Coronada Beach, Florida. He holds the enviable record of forty-nine successive seasons of sailing on the Great Lakes without a serious mishap.

Born into a family already deep in lake transportation, "Billie" Benham soon learned how to navigate sailing ships from his father, Captain Charles E. Benham, who owned a considerable fleet of schooners and tugs. Naturally, young "Billie" took to the water and, as a boy, he sailed in his father's windjammers and learned the ways of the lakes. At twenty years of age he received his first command, the schooner *Henry C. Richards*.

As the steamer superseded sail, the youthful Captain Benham transferred his attentions to the former, although he still believes that a real sailor should know something about sails. Today, a natty sail boat, for pleasure only, is tied to the Benham pier at "South Anchorage" in the Halifax River in Florida.

One of the early outstanding steamers commanded by Captain Benham was the *City of Glasgow*. This staunch wooden ship of the 1890's was the father of all the trim ships that today comprise the fleet of Hutchinson & Company. The *City of Glasgow* is reported to have been Captain Charles L. Hutchinson's first purchase in what eventually became the Pioneer Steamship Company fleet, which is managed by Hutchinson & Company, and Captain Benham was given command of the ship.

The *City of Glasgow* proved a success and was exceptionally fast. Her former skipper recalls that, on one particular occasion, he made the run from Detour, Michigan, to Port Huron, Michigan, in twenty-one hours and forty minutes with the barge *Abyssinia* in tow. Good time for a ship of today! The barge *Abyssinia* was added to the young fleet. The *City of Glasgow* became a familiar sight along the lake lanes as she towed the *Abyssinia*.

Another interesting old freighter that Captain Benham commanded was the wooden *Yakima*, which boat is said to have been the first to carry electric lights on the Great Lakes. These lights were of the arc-light type, and two of them were mounted on the boiler house and cast their sputtering rays upon the deck.

As senior captain in the matured Pioneer Steamship fleet he brought out the freighters: *Ravenscraig; Martin Mullen* in 1904; *W. A. Paine* in 1905; *Joseph G. Butler, Jr.,* now the *Donald B. Gillies,* in 1905; *J. J. Sullivan* in

237

1907 and later the ill-fated *John A. McGean,* from the builders' shipyards.

Captain Benham recalls that, on the first trip of the new *Joseph G. Butler, Jr.,* he ran into one of the stiffest "blows" in his career. He also ran through the terrible "Big Storm" of 1913. He sighted the overturned steamer *Charles S. Price* at the lower end of Lake Huron but saw no wreckage. The extreme dangers encountered on that trip, when many vessels near him were sent to their doom, is quietly passed over by the white haired veteran, who considers it "just another good stiff blow."

A brother of Captain Benham's was lost on the lakes. Captain G. E. Benham perished with his crew when his ship, the *John Owen,* foundered in a raging gale off Caribou Island in Lake Superior in 1919.

An interesting speed run for large freighters was made by the steamer *Philip D. Block* under Captain Benham. The big ship sailed from Buffalo during the night of December eighth, about ten years ago, without cargo, for Fort William, Ontario, the Canadian head of the Great Lakes. In the remarkably short time of six days, the *Block* returned to Buffalo heavily laden with wheat. Considering the lateness of the season, with its consequent bad sailing weather, and the time required to load the big cargo, the *Block* made an exceptionally fast trip, averaging some thirteen and one-half miles per hour while enroute. Captain Benham commanded the *Philip D. Block* for ten seasons.

Figures compiled on the total bulk cargo movement on

the Great Lakes in recent years are very interesting. A table of such follows:

BULK CARGO MOVEMENT ON THE GREAT LAKES

Year	Iron Ore	Coal	Grain	Stone	Total
1938	21,574,572	34,623,287	10,679,125	8,240,768	75,117,752
1937	70,110,696	44,318,765	5,829,399	14,429,379	134,688,239
1936	50,200,666	44,699,443	7,433,967	12,080,672	114,414,748
1935	31,765,852	35,289,135	6,750,261	9,082,155	82,887,403
1934	24,919,552	35,476,575	7,951,145	7,392,218	75,739,490
1933	24,218,766	31,776,654	8,713,127	6,664,629	71,373,176
1932	3,996,143	24,857,369	8,893,409	3,928,840	41,675,761
1929	73,029,152	39,254,578	10,021,099	16,269,612	138,574,441

In 1932 this great inland water transportation industry was prostrated. Since that time there has been a steady increase in traffic on the lakes with the year 1937 coming very close to 1929 in total tonnage. However, due to the abrupt decline in the steel business, with its subsequent low rate of operation creating a large ore carry-over, 1938 was the worst year with the exception of 1932, since the year 1900. Coal was near the ten-year average tonnage. Grain—while a much larger movement of grain is shown above, this source was offset to some extent by adverse freight rates. Figures for the 1939 season were not available at the time this book went to press, but it is presumed that they will exceed, in all commodities, the figures for 1938.

Army engineers' statistical report on 1936 traffic through the Detroit River shows that stream to be the busiest of any in the world. During that year it is reported that, exclusive of passages between foreign ports, vessel passages totaled 18,193 with 61,826,844 tons of freight worth $868,364,123. This was a sharp decline from the year previous which showed $1,202,118,225.

LORE OF THE LAKES

A list of American Great Lakes ore carriers for 1938 arranged according to fleets and showing their carrying capacity on a draft of nineteen feet is as follows:

THE 1938 LIST OF AMERICAN GREAT LAKES ORE BOAT FLEETS

Fleet	Number of Ships	Capacity Per Trip	Average Size
Pittsburgh Steamship Company	79	715,400	9,056
Interlake Steamship Company	45	397,200	8,827
Hutchinson & Co., Managers	22	190,500	8,659
Cleveland Cliffs Iron Company	24	185,300	7,721
Bethlehem Transportation Company	16	159,400	9,963
Great Lakes Steamship Company	19	144,300	7,595
Wilson Transit Company	13	111,600	8,585
Columbia Transportation Company	14	107,200	7,657
The M. A. Hanna Co., Agents	11	104,500	9,500
G. A. Tomlinson	10	85,400	8,540
Reiss Steamship Company	10	80,900	8,090
Boland & Cornelius	8	62,200	7,775
Buckeye Steamship Company	11	59,000	5,364
Midland Steamship Company	7	54,600	7,800
Interstate Steamship Company	4	40,600	10,150
H. & G. M. Steinbrenner	4	35,500	8,875
Shenango Steamship Company	3	34,400	11,467
Ford Motor Company	2	21,800	10,900
Wisconsin Steel Company	2	20,800	10,400
D. Sullivan & Company	2	15,600	7,800
Brown & Company	2	14,000	7,000
	308	2,640,200	8,572
Previous year (1937)	304	2,594,600	8,535

Chapter Seventeen

TODAY'S PASSENGER FLEET

One can board a trim passenger ship on any of the five Great Lakes and enjoy the delights of water travel, be his journey that of a few hours, a few days, or a couple of weeks. Lake passenger travel today is one of the safest forms of transportation. Strict laws governing the ships, the equipment aboard, and the men who sail them, are rigidly enforced by the United States Government. The cost of such a trip is small indeed for all that one receives. The boats are clean and the cuisine is equal to that of any good hotel or salt water ship. Whatever the duration of the vacation—a day or a week—it can be well spent by traveling on our great inland seas.

Many excursion steamers make a one-day round trip from the larger lake cities to some enchanting resort along the shore; to an island or even to another city. The change of scenery from the crowded city to the broad openness of the water is always relaxing and refreshing. The air is clean and exhilarating. Almost any combination of journey can be fitted into a lake cruise, and for any number of days. Canada always affords an interesting visit, while the northern lakes still offer much in the way of wild ruggedness to the traveler desiring something different.

Nowhere in the world will be found such a fleet of excursion boats and pleasure cruises as is to be found on the

241

Great Lakes. In most cases the ships have been built for the particular trip on which they operate. They are well suited for the convenience and comfort of their passengers.

Outstanding in this is the steamer *Put-in-Bay* of the Ashley and Dustin Line. Leaving Detroit on its regular run, this well appointed ship cruises down the Detroit River to Put-In-Bay Island and Sandusky, passing first the busy shore-line of the city on the starboard side with the interesting border of Canada on the port side. The passing ship traffic, close enough to hail, is intensely interesting; a never ending parade of freight vessels, many from far away foreign lands, with cargoes that stagger the imagination: ore, coal, grain, stone, automobiles, butter, eggs, fruit, blue-berries, liquors, newsprint, gasoline, oil; in fact almost everything imaginable is water borne. At the mouth of the Detroit River, twenty miles below Detroit, the steamer *Put-In-Bay* enters Lake Erie, and the shore line fades into the distance. The famous Lake Erie Islands soon come into view, the first being Middle Sister Island in Canadian waters.

Near this spot the ships of Great Britain and the United States met in bloody combat and fought the great Battle of Lake Erie in 1813. A sixty minute further sail brings the *Put-In-Bay* to the island for which the ship was named. The public generally knows the island as Put-in-Bay, but the real name of the island is South Bass Island; however, this name is all but lost in the old time charts and maps. Many passengers disembark here and enjoy the pleasures of this enchanting island and await the return of their ship later in the afternoon for the run back to Detroit.

TODAY'S PASSENGER FLEET

The island itself contains one thousand seven hundred and fifty acres and has a permanent population whose homes cluster about the quaint little town close to the wharf. Seen towering high against the sky is the gigantic Doric shaft of the Perry Memorial Monument, built of Milford granite, three hundred fifty-two feet high, forty-five feet wide at the base and thirty-five feet at the peak. Its walls are almost ten feet thick at the base and five feet thick at the peak. Architecturally, this imposing mass of enduring beauty is regarded as one of the finest memorials in the United States and ranks high among the world's commemorative monuments. It was unveiled September 10, 1913, on the one-hundredth anniversary of Commodore Perry's victory. The open air promenade at the top, accommodating three hundred people, is reached by an elevator, where is enjoyed a view of unequalled beauty over a land and water area of fifty miles, taking in the Lake Erie Islands, the Canadian shore to the north and the Ohio shore to the south.

This enduring memorial, erected by the United States Government and the States of Ohio, Pennsylvania, Michigan, Wisconsin, New York, Rhode Island, Kentucky, Illinois and Massachusetts, commemorates a century of peace between Canada and the United States. It towers skyward in noble tribute to the Treaty of 1817 providing for the limitation of armament of the Great Lakes. Its cost exceeded one million dollars. Several bodies of sailors who died during the Battle of Lake Erie are buried at the base of the shaft.

The steamer *Put-In-Bay* continues on her run, passing close to many interesting islands, among which are Kel-

243

ley's Island and Johnson's Island. The terminal of the trip is the city of Sandusky, Ohio. This port is busy with freighters transporting coal, sand, stone, fish and fruit cargoes. Here connections can be made with the ferry steamer *G. A. Boeckling* for Cedar Point, and the Canadian ship *Erie Isles* for Pelee Island and Leamington, Ontario.

From Sandusky, an excursion run to the Lake Erie Islands is covered by two small vessels making daily runs. This service formerly was made by the steamer *City of Hancock,* which has since been transferred to Lake Superior.

In Sandusky Bay is located Johnson's Island, consisting of about two hundred and seventy-five acres, the site of a Union Prison during the Civil War. From the period of its establishment until the close of the war it is estimated that about fifteen thousand soldiers were confined there. Owing to its supposed security, the prisoners were largely composed of Southern officers. Over two hundred officers of the South still rest in this little island cemetery. This Confederate Cemetery, for years cared for by the Daughters of the Confederacy, is visited annually by many.

The stately ship, *Put-In-Bay*, heads from Sandusky on its return run to the island of Put-In-Bay, where a short stop is made and the trip back to Detroit is continued.

The steamer *Put-In-Bay*, owned and operated by the Ashley and Dustin Steamer Line, and captained by John N. Peterson, is one of the largest and most costly day excursion steamers on the Great Lakes. Designed by the famous marine architect, Frank E. Kirby, ably assisted by the Dustin brothers, who gave him the benefit of their years of experience on the run, the ship was built to fit exactly the demands of this trip.

The sidewheel type of ship was abandoned for the propeller type. Another innovation was the construction of a hardwood floor on the ballroom deck. Many marine men were of the opinion that the floor would buckle and give rise to considerable trouble, but nothing of the kind ever happened and the grand ballroom floor is in as good condition today as it was when the steamer first came out.

The hull of the *Put-In-Bay* and the main deck are constructed of iron, thus cutting off the boiler room and kitchens from the wooden superstructure. On the main deck there is a splendid water sprinkler system, and here and all over the boat are fire alarm boxes placed at strategic points. This alarm system is connected with the Detroit still alarm system when the boat is at the dock in Detroit.

In the iron hull of the steamer are placed several watertight bulkheads which were thought by Engineer Kirby ample to make the boat unsinkable, but recently to make the factor of safety greater than ever, Mr. Dustin has placed another bulkhead in the midship part of the hold. This steamer has everything right up to date that tends to insure the safety and comfort of the passengers.

Passengers, boarding the *Put-In-Bay*, find themselves on the main deck in the forward portion of the ship, close to the grand stairway that leads to the ballroom deck. At the stern is a commodious dining room where patrons may enjoy serve-self or waiter service.

Immediately above the main deck is the huge ballroom deck which is so ample that hundreds may find seats and hundreds more enjoy themselves on the dancing floor. This fine room occupies the full length and width of the ship and is glass enclosed.

On the deck above the ballroom is located the observation parlor in the forward part of the ship. Straight ahead and on both sides the view is unobstructed. Back of the observation parlor is located a number of private parlors which can accommodate five or more people.

The ship carries two thousand eight hundred day passengers in comfort, and has a crew of one hundred and ten officers and men. She is two hundred fifty-six feet long and sixty feet beam, with a draft of thirteen feet six inches. The *Put-In-Bay* is equipped with a four cylinder triple expansion engine, which develops three thousand horsepower and gives the ship a speed of twenty miles per hour. She was built by the American Shipbuilding Company.

Two other pleasure steamers operate out of Detroit. These are the oil-fueled *Columbia* and *Ste. Claire,* especially adapted for operation in the waters about the city of Detroit. They make daily excursion trips to Bob-Lo Island. In the evenings they carry many Detroiters on moonlight excursions where dancing and relief from the heat of a big city is offered.

A steamer ferry service is maintained between Detroit

and Walkerville, Ontario, for the accommodation of pedestrians and motor vehicles.

Lake excursion enthusiasts in Buffalo turn to the steamer *Canadiana* for their diversion on Lake Erie. This ship operates between Buffalo and Crystal Beach on the Canadian shore, about ten miles distant.

The once vast fleet of excursion and pleasure steamers that operated out of Chicago has now dwindled to but two ships. These are the steamers *Theodore Roosevelt*, which runs from that port to Benton Harbor and South Haven, Michigan, and the *City of Grand Rapids* which runs to Milwaukee, Wisconsin. Both ships are on daily schedule during the season and leave from the Navy Pier.

Overnight runs are popular with the lake steamers. They are enjoyed by the business man who is anxious to partake of the lake atmosphere, and also the automobile tourist who places his car aboard, anxious to be off the busy highway and to relax on deck. Such trips can be made between Cleveland and Detroit, and between Detroit and Buffalo. Overnight trips can also be arranged between various ports aboard the regular cruise ships making the entire run of the lakes.

The Lake Michigan carferries have excellent accommodations for passengers and motor vehicles across the lake. Popular on these runs are the Pere Marquette fast automobile ferries from Ludington, Michigan, to Kewaunee, Manitowoc, and Milwaukee, on the Wisconsin shore. These ferries permit motorists to avoid the long drive around the base of Lake Michigan, and they operate daily service throughout the year, weather permitting. This fleet, of which the *City of Saginaw 31* is at present the flagship, is composed of electrically-driven steel steamers that are among the largest and finest of their type on the Great Lakes, each with ample storage facilities for automobiles, trucks and trailers. Built to carry passengers as well as motor vehicles, these ferries offer luxurious accommodations and excellent cuisine. Commodious private staterooms with hot and cold running water and perfect ventilation are available.

Other ferries in this fleet are: the *City of Flint—32;* and several carrying the name *Pere Marquette* with the number of the ship, such as: *12; 14; 17; 18; 19; 21 and 22.*

A carferry of this fleet, the number *20,* was, in 1938, sold to the Michigan Highway Commission. It was extensively rebuilt and converted into a Straits of Mackinac automobile and passenger ferry and renamed the *City of Munising.*

A new and streamlined carferry is at present being constructed for this fleet at the shipyards of the Manitowoc Shipbuilding Company. It is reported to cost in the vicinity of two million dollars and will be the largest and most powerful of its type of lake ship, being four hundred and six feet long, with a beam of fifty-seven feet and molded depth of twenty-three and one-half feet.

The Ann Arbor Railroad Company operates a fleet of carferries on Lake Michigan between the ports of Frankfort, Mich., and Menominee, Mich., Kewaunee, Wis., Manistique, Mich., Manitowoc, Wis.

TODAY'S PASSENGER FLEET

These ships operate the year round regardless of weather conditions, and have excellent accommodations for passenger and automobiles. These include cabins, staterooms, parlors, dining room, radio, and other up-to-date conveniences for the safety and comfort of tourists.

Mackinac Island has long been a focal point for passenger steamer travel. Many short excursion trips start from here. The small steamer *Mackinac Islander* operates to the Les Cheneaux Islands, a beautiful ride through winding channels between wooded islands with Cedarville, Michigan, as the terminal. Steamer service is also maintained from Mackinac Island to Saint Ignace and Cheboygan. The steamer *Algomah II* operates in the Straits between Mackinac Island and the mainland points of Mackinaw City and Cheboygan.

Approximately one-third of Michigan lies above the Straits of Mackinac, and two-thirds forms the "lower peninsula" or mainland. State owned and operated ferry service across the Straits commenced in 1923. A tremendous volume of traffic has developed since its inception, as shown by the facts that during the first year of operation these ferries carried a few more than ten thousand vehicles, while during 1938 they transported almost one-quarter of a million vehicles.

The present fleet consists of six vessels: the *City of Munising; City of Cheboygan; Mackinaw City; Straits of Mackinac; Sainte Ignace;* and the carferry *Sainte Marie,* which operates under charter. Efficient terminals facilitate the fast loading and unloading of these busy ships They maintain year around service.

The flagship, *City of Munising,* was formerly the *Pere Marquette 20,* operated as a railroad ferry on Lake Michigan, as previously mentioned. She has an overall length of three hundred and thirty-nine feet, and is the largest in the state-owned fleet. She has a capacity of one hundred and fifteen to one hundred and twenty vehicles, compared to eighty-five for the next largest ferry, the *City of Cheboygan.*

A most delightful vacation can be spent on a cruise of the entire length of the Great Lakes. The sleek lake liners *North American, South American* and *Alabama* of the Chicago, Duluth and Georgian Bay Line, make these trips. The *North American* and the *South American* have been making the run from Buffalo to Chicago, while the *Alabama* has run from Buffalo to Duluth, with a special stop at Isle Royale in Lake Superior. The *North American* and *South American* make stops at several points in Georgian Bay. These three ships are all painted a spotless white and are very well kept up.

The *North American* and the *South American* are called "the ocean liners of the lakes." These oil-fueled ships have neat, airy staterooms and deluxe bedrooms, all outside, facing the water; spacious decks; carpeted promenade encircling the ship; as well as sun and observation decks. Each ship has accommodation for about five hundred passengers, with ample sports and entertainment facilities. No freight is carried. Complete safety equipment includes automatic sprinkler system, gyroscopic and magnetic compasses, radio direction finders, and two way wireless.

250

TODAY'S PASSENGER FLEET

The big ship *Seeandbee* makes the cruise from Buffalo to Chicago, stoping at Cleveland, Detroit, Mackinac Island and the Soo. The entire round trip requires one week. This ship is described in detail elsewhere in this book. Safety equipment of the *Seeandbee* meets the most rigid government inspection requirements, including an automatic sprinkler system throughout the ship. Staterooms are comfortable, each with double lower berth and single upper berth. All rooms have hot and cold water, and telephone. A washed air ventilating system, with forced draft, assures the comfort and airiness of all inside staterooms.

The steamer *Georgian* of Seaway Lines operates cruises from Detroit to points on Georgian Bay, including Parry Sound, Killarney and Manitoulin Island, which is claimed to be the largest island in the world that is surrounded by fresh water. These are very interesting cruises into ports not usually touched by the lake passenger boats. Features of the *Georgian* include: all staterooms with large windows and outside exposure; exceptionally large public rooms, all located on the upper deck away from the staterooms; no promenade around the stateroom decks, so complete privacy is assured; twin screw propulsion which eliminates vibration.

The Detroit and Cleveland Navigation Company, whose main offices are in Detroit, operates a fleet of six sidewheel steamers, two of which are the largest passenger ships at present on the Great Lakes. These are the twin steamers *Greater Detroit* and *Greater Buffalo*, and they are the newest vessels of the fleet. They cross Lake Erie

251

nightly between Detroit and Buffalo. Each of these vessels is reported to have cost three and one-half million dollars to build. Each has sleeping accommodations for one thousand seven hundred passengers and for a crew of two hundred and seventy-five. They were built at Lorain and Detroit in 1924.

The D & C steamers *City of Detroit III* and *City of Cleveland III* operate nightly service between the cities of Detroit and Cleveland, carrying passengers and freight. These ships appear to be twins to the casual observer; however, the *City of Detroit III* is the larger of the two, though their services to the traveling public are practically identical.

The two other D & C steamers, *Eastern States* and *Western States,* are twin ships. For a few years they maintained passenger and freight service between Detroit and Chicago, but this division was dropped about 1938. The *Eastern States* operates an excursion run between Cleveland and Cedar Point, Ohio.

FACTS ABOUT THE D & C FLEET

Steamer	Passenger Capacity	Gross Tonnage	Length Overall	Beam Overall	Dining Room Capacity	State Rooms	Crew
Greater Detroit	2127	7739	536 ft.	96 ft.	375	625	275
Greater Buffalo	2127	7739	536 ft.	96 ft.	375	625	275
City of Detroit III	1440	6061	470 ft.	93 ft.	270	435	230
City of Cleveland III	1451	4568	402 ft.	91½ ft.	225	390	225
Eastern States	735	3077	362 ft.	80 ft.	175	209	175
Western States	735	3077	362 ft.	80 ft.	175	209	175

The ships of the D & C fleet are all painted with a black hull and cream superstructure, with all black stacks, and are well officered and well maintained.

252

TODAY'S PASSENGER FLEET

The steamers *Noronic* and *Hamonic,* of the Northern Navigation Division of the Canadian Steamship Lines, operate a most interesting cruise of seven days from Detroit to Duluth with stops at the Canadian ports of Sarnia, Soo, Port Arthur and Fort William. The *Noronic* is said to be the largest cruise ship on the lakes of the propeller type. She is the flagship of the fleet and is almost four hundred feet long; has six decks; stateroom accommodations for five hundred and sixty-two passengers; dining salon on the observation deck, seating two hundred and seventy-two persons. The *Hamonic,* which is slightly smaller, has all the attractive features which are found on the *Noronic.* All the staterooms are comfortable and commodious, some with beds instead of berths, some with bath, and all with running water. These ships have: barber shops; smoking rooms; buffet bars; music rooms; writing rooms; observation rooms, used as ballrooms during the evening; and beautiful dining salons with wide observation windows, which permit views of passing scenes from every seat.

A never-to-be-forgotten cruise is the one offered by the Canada Steamship Lines to the Saguenay River and Eastern Canada. This cruise stops at the cities of Niagara Falls, Toronto, Rochester, the Thousand Islands, the Rapids, Montreal, Quebec and the Saguenay River with its towering capes "Trinity" and "Eternity." This cruise is made in several ships of the Canada Steamship Lines and ample shore stops are made. This trip usually requires about ten days time, depending on the point of embarkation.

LORE OF THE LAKES

In the Canadian Pacific passenger fleet on the Great Lakes are the steamers *Assiniboia* and *Keewatin*. These trim white-sided Clyde-built steamships maintain a convenient service between Port McNicoll and Fort William for the passenger and freight trade.

There is no finer trip anywhere in the world than between these ports on one of these staunch steamers, a distance of five hundred and forty-two miles over an enchanting lake and river route. Sailings are made semiweekly during the season. Summer cruises are also operated from Port McNicoll and Owen Sound by the steamer *Manitoba*. The *Assiniboia* and *Keewatin* are three hundred and fifty feet in length, forty-three feet in breadth, and fifteen foot depth. They have a speed of fifteen knots, with gross tonnage of three thousand eight hundred and eighty tons, and net tonnage of two thousand four hundred and eighty-six tons. All rooms have running water and lights in each berth. The dancing and observation lounge has large observation windows, lounge facilities and polished oak dance floor.

The Canadian motor ship *Midland City* operates a most enchanting run among the Thirty Thousand Islands of Georgian Bay, having Parry Sound and Midland, Ontario, as terminals. The *Midland City* cruises the "inside route" not available to the ordinary lake steamer. On many of the channels the ship wends its way so close to land that one might almost step ashore. Picturesque island rock formations, green wooded islands and winding channels, diverging in all directions, make the Thirty Thousand Island cruise one long to be remembered.

TODAY'S PASSENGER FLEET

The trim white side-wheel steamer *Montauk* operates excursions and sight-seeing trips from Duluth and Fond du Lac. The *Montauk* is especially suitable for this run. It is one hundred and ninety feet long, has three decks of fifty-five feet breadth, is allowed one thousand and seventy day passengers and has a maximum speed of eighteen miles per hour. A trip aboard the *Montauk* is both instructive and historic, offering the best way to see the busy harbor traffic of the twin ports of Duluth and Superior, and also the old Indian country along the picturesque Saint Louis River to Fond du Lac, the very head of navigation of the Great Lakes.

Countless millions of travelers and vacationers have enjoyed themselves upon the refreshing waters of our Great Lakes. Countless others will find their way to the ships that offer relaxation, travel, adventure and entertainment upon these lakes. Owners of the passenger ships will see that the traveler on their vessels is given every comfort and convenience that water travel anywhere in the world affords.

Great thriving cities have sprung up along the shores of the Great Lakes, but the lakes themselves are still as nature made them, unspoiled by the hand of man.

⚓ ⚓ ⚓ ⚓ ⚓ ⚓ ⚓ ⚓

Chapter Eighteen

THE PASSENGER STEAMER SEEANDBEE

How well I recall my first view of the giant passenger steamer of the lakes, the *Seeandbee!* I was driving along Lake Erie's shore in Gordon Park at Cleveland late one summer afternoon. I had stopped to admire the view, when I saw the big freshwater side-wheeler entering the east entrance of the Cleveland breakwater.

What a sight she was! She came in close enough for me to see her every detail. I could easily see her passengers relaxing on the decks. I had never before beheld such a large passenger ship. In fact there were few larger to be seen on salt water, and none on the lakes. It was the summer of 1913.

The giant ship seemed to be just too big to float on water. She was as long as a city block and appeared to be wider than the widest street I had ever seen. Deck after deck stood out above the water line, with hundreds of stateroom windows flashing in her white cabin walls.

Her four great smokestacks belched forth volumes of velvety black smoke that drifted lazily over the water. To this day there is no other ship that sails the lakes that can boast of four stacks. Her pilot house, like the ship itself, was the largest I had ever seen, and as she moved majestically along, I could see the white capped uniformed men inside, peering ahead through the lowered windows, and the man at the wheel, steering the great ship.

The *Seeandbee* had just come out that season, and she was the talk of the lakes. Everyone who saw her marveled at her greatness. She was the undisputed "Queen of the Lakes."

Equally well remembered is my first trip aboard the *Seeandbee*. It was made over one Labor Day about 1915, from Cleveland to Buffalo and return. The summer holidays were always gala events aboard the lake steamers, and this occasion was outstanding. Every stateroom and berth on the giant ship was occupied, and the overflow of passengers was accommodated for the overnight trip in the cabins. Entire families could be seen draped over the cabin chairs or lying prone on the thickly carpeted floors. After the ship was well out in the lake and the more fortunate stateroom passengers had retired, the ship's watchman had to step carefully in going his rounds about the darkened cabins to avoid stepping on some sleeping passenger that was sprawled in what he thought was a secure spot for the night. Lake passenger travel was still at a high level.

The *Seeandbee* is at present writing, one of the three largest passenger ships that ply the Great Lakes. From the time of her launching at Wyandotte, Michigan, on November 9, 1912, until 1925, when the ships *Greater Detroit* and *Greater Buffalo* were built, the *Seeandbee* held undisputed claim as the largest sidewheel steamer in the world, besides being the most costly passenger ship afloat on the lakes. Her keel length of 485 feet is ex-

257

ceeded on the lakes only by the twin steamers *Greater Detroit* and *Greater Buffalo,* whose keel lengths are each 519 feet. The hull beam of all three ships is the same, fifty-eight feet, as is the depth, which is twenty-three feet, seven inches. The *Seeandbee* has the widest deck beam of any ship on the lakes, and exceeds that of many ocean liners. She measures ninety-eight feet six inches over guards, while the *Greater Detroit* and *Greater Buffalo* measure ninety-six feet. The *Queen Mary's* beam is one hundred and eighteen feet.

During the season of 1913 the *Seeandbee* entered the run for which she was originally built, between Cleveland and Buffalo, primarily as a night boat. Daylight trips were made when the demand warranted.

The ship is palatial. Upon going aboard, one enters the spacious lobby on the main deck. Here are located the purser's and steward's offices, telephone switchboard, check room and other shipboard necessities. The main dining room is located just aft of the grand salon and affords the diner a full view of the water. Forward of the lobby are located the large engine room and freight deck. Above the main deck are three decks devoted mostly to staterooms and parlors. In the center of the ship, for almost its entire length, and opening onto three decks, is the grand salon. The atrium, with its comfortable chairs, is located on the upper deck aft. A large ball room and a beautiful cocktail lounge are located on the upper deck, affording the passenger an excellent view outdoors. The woodwork in cabins and halls is of a rich mahogany and ivory.

THE PASSENGER STEAMER SEEANDBEE

At the suggestion of many passengers who wished to spend more time aboard the palatial ship than her regular overnight run permitted, a cruise at the close of her Cleveland-Buffalo season was inaugurated in 1921. This cruise was truly an extraordinary one and a gala affair. Passenger list was limited to five hundred, a mere handful on such a large ship. Everything possible was done by the Cleveland & Buffalo Transit Company, the owners, to make the trip one of pleasure and relaxation. It was rather late in the season for lake cruising, as the trip started about September twelfth and returned five days later, but the early fall weather is enchanting on the lower lakes. In the daytime the air is bracing and in the evening there was always entertainment to be had inside.

The author was aboard the *Seeandbee* in 1922 on her second annual cruise, and several subsequent ones. The first cruise was such a success that the line decided to run the event each year at the same time. In looking over my mementoes of the second annual trip, I find the advertising literature, itinerary, passenger list and photographs very interesting. In one of the folders, I find the following:

"For this Lake Cruise DeLuxe, every want and comfort of the guest is provided for on the Great Ship *Seeandbee*. This, combined with an itinerary offering many scenes of beauty and interest, assures the guest of a most delightful and restful cruise.

"Spacious staterooms equipped with wide and comfortable berths, running water, telephone, and electric lights, luxurious parlor rooms, some with private balconies overlooking the water, private baths, brass bedsteads, snowy linen and soft downy blankets, give all the comforts of the most modern hotel. The Great Ship is, in fact, a great hotel afloat.

"A corps of courteous attendants awaits your call to serve you with every desirable comfort.

"The delicious meals are served in the big Main Dining Room overlooking the water.

"The Grand Saloon, Lounge and Buffet provide supreme comforts and conveniences.

"The Grand Saloon is a magnificent room more than 400 feet long. On its lofty ceiling is a great mural painting of rare beauty and design. The carpets are of thick rich velvet. Chairs and lounges give it the luxurious comfort of a great drawing room.

"The Lounge and the Atrium, with windows overlooking the water, are other attractive features of the Great Ship. The former is finished in Flemish oak, with tables and chairs covered with Spanish leather. The decorative scheme of the Atrium gives an out-of-doors effect which is most appealing.

"The Great Ship *Seeandbee* is the largest and most costly steamer on inland waters of the world, 500 feet long, 98 feet 6 inches broad, 500 staterooms and twenty-four parlors.

"In beauty of interior decoration and completeness of appointments the Great Ship is as notable as for size. The rich woodwork, the beautiful mural paintings, the convenience and the spaciousness of the ship are constant sources of wonderment, even to those who have traveled on her again and again.

THE PASSENGER STEAMER SEEANDBEE

"Cruising on this large floating palace is a most fascinating experience. Its spacious decks and the richness of its interior appointments make it especially delightful with a party of only 500 guests aboard."

The itinerary of this cruise called for leaving Cleveland on Monday, September 11th, at midnight. Tuesday was consumed in "a delightful daylight cruise up the Detroit River, passing Detroit at 7 A. M.; through Lake St. Clair, passing Port Huron at 11 A. M. and thence up Lake Huron." Wednesday was "another interesting daylight cruise through the picturesque St. Mary's River, reaching Sault Ste. Marie at 1 P. M., with the remainder of the day and evening at these famous canal locks."

As the *Seeandbee* wended her way, marine salutes of three long and two short blasts of the whistle and answers in the same manner, were almost constant, as she steamed stately up the Detroit, the Saint Clair and the Saint Mary's Rivers. Every ship and shore plant saluted the new "Queen of the Lakes." Smiling his happiness in being her commander, the jovial Captain Hugh McAlpine answered all the salutes by pulling the whistle cord on his ship and sending out across the waters a deep pleasant tone of thanks for the welcome.

Below the great Soo Locks, the *Seeandbee* laid over that night. It is not possible for her to go through the locks, due to her great width. During the evening there, open house was held for anyone wishing to come aboard. Hundreds came, many from miles away, all marine minded. They swarmed over the ship like bees. All agreed that the *Seeandbee* exceeded their greatest expectations.

On the next day, Thursday, September fourteenth, our itinerary called for "Leaving Sault Ste. Marie at 7 A. M., and arriving at Mackinac Island at 1 P. M. Five hours to stay on this beautiful island—ample time to view its famous old fort and other historical features. Leave Mackinac Island at 6 P. M."

The folder continued, "Friday, arrive at Detroit at 12 noon. Ten and one-half hours in the 'City of the Straits' —ample time for sight-seeing trips to Belle Isle; Windsor, Canada; and the many large automobile manufacturing plants. Leave Detroit at 10:30 P. M."

As the big ship steamed down Lake Huron toward the rivers and Detroit, I recall an incident in radio, which was at that time very much in its infancy. Notice was posted that the wireless operator would attempt to hold a radio concert in the grand saloon that morning. He had learned that music was to be played as an experiment for broadcasting in Detroit. So, our enthusiastic wireless operator decided to try to receive it. Interest ran high among the passengers and crew. Many wires were strung from the wireless room to the grand saloon and a great amount of preliminary work took place before the concert started. We all assembled at the appointed hour to hear the concert broadcast. I am quite sure that few of those aboard had as yet ever heard a radio broadcast. I had heard music over small individual headphones, but never in volume enough for all in a room to hear. This surely would be something to tell the folks back home. The time

262

arrived, but all was not well with the reception. The wireless operator's face was real red as he struggled with this gadget and that, only to produce unearthly squeals and squawks and a great amount of code. Once in a while, we would catch a few strains of music and we would all be delighted. We had actually heard music come out of the air! Many scoffed at the poor reception attempt, but most all agreed that they believed "they had something there."

Cleveland, and the end of the cruise, was reached early on Saturday, September sixteenth. Passengers left the ship enthusiastic over the cruise.

These cruise trips proved to be so popular that the ship was later put into cruise service exclusively, and at present writing, the *Seeandbee* is engaged in such cruise service. She has a very interesting itinerary and has been remodeled some to better accommodate cruise travel.

Thousands upon thousands of people have traveled aboard the *Seeandbee,* and countless thousands will continue to enjoy its pleasures. Many long and worthwhile friendships are made aboard ship, where in the carefree atmosphere on deck, one chats freely with his fellow cruisers, and there are formed the foundations for real and lasting friendships.

How many more years the *Seeandbee* will ply the lakes is anyone's guess. It is not unusual for a well-kept-up ship to last forty to fifty years. Constant repairs keep a boat in first-class condition. Lake steamers last much longer than do their salt water cousins, because their season of operation is only about two or three months per

263

year, while the ship on salt water is quite likely to operate the entire twelve months. Then, too, the action of the
salt water on the hull, and in fact on all parts of a ship, is
a great deal more devastating than is the fresh water of
the lakes. The salt water ship is subjected to a great
amount of detrimental water life, such as the barnacle.
This shell fish will cling in great numbers to a ship's bottom and sides, and must be periodically removed by
scraping.

Rust is the great destroyer of ships but, while it does
cause considerable damage to ships of the Great Lakes, it
is not to be compared with the rust that attacks the ships
of salt water. Marine men say that the average life of
a well-kept-up salt water ship is around twenty to thirty
years.

Obsolescence is also a factor in sea-going ships, as the
traveling public favors the newest and latest in ships as in
almost everything else.

Since beginning her career, the *Seeandbee* has had but
three masters. Captain Hugh McAlpine brought her out
and sailed her for several years. At his death, Captain
Neil J. McPhail took over her command. Captain Mc-
Phail sailed this "Queen of the Lakes" several years when
Captain Allen Strachan took over the command, and is
the present master of the vessel.

In charge of her engine room when she came out was
Chief Engineer Charles Lorimer. Upon his retirement
from the lakes, George Turnbull took over the engine
room, and upon his promotion to superintendent of the
line, he was succeeded by William H. Caine. William
Robinson is her present chief engineer.

THE PASSENGER STEAMER SEEANDBEE

Occasionally a ship will have a man in her crew that will remain with the ship during her entire active life. So far, the *Seeandbee* has such a man, Ernest Blanchard, an engineer. He was in her engine room when the big ship first cleared Wyandotte, where she was built, and has been at her controls each season since, save 1932, when the ship lay idle at Cleveland.

It is no wonder that to such a man his ship becomes a part of him. Its good fortune is shared by him, as is its misfortune. Stability is a great virtue whether it be in a man or a ship.

⚓ ⚓ ⚓ ⚓ ⚓ ⚓ ⚓ ⚓

CHAPTER NINETEEN

THE BURNING OF THE STEAMER CITY OF BUFFALO

No one will ever know exactly just what happened aboard the Cleveland & Buffalo Line passenger steamer *City of Buffalo* between the minutes of 6:10 and 6:45 on the dark morning of March 20, 1938. More than a million people soon learned the result. The venerable forty-two-year-old "honeymoon special" burned to a total loss as she was tied to her winter moorings at the East Ninth Street Pier in Cleveland.

It was at 6:10 A. M. that her night watchman left the boat to go to his home, and all was well aboard. Thirty-five minutes later her day watchman arrived. Reports are that he found the electric lights flickering, but nothing else was amiss. He made his rounds of the nearby C & B ships, *City of Erie* and *Seeandbee,* and returned to the *City of Buffalo.*

The lights still flickered. He went aft to investigate but was unable to detect the cause. Several more rounds of the ships were made and about eighty-thirty he smelled smoke coming from the after part of the main deck near the dining room. He ran ashore and called the Cleveland Fire Department.

By the time the first fireman reached the ship, the flames were high above her top deck. As the vessel was in winter quarters, and therefore not in commission at the

266

time, all her own fire extinguishing apparatus was disconnected and not in service.

Workmen had been preparing her for the coming summer lake season for her usual run between Cleveland and Buffalo. Possibly they had left oily rags that had ignited, or a cigar or cigarette stub left carelessly had not been extinguished, or a defect in the electric wiring had developed. The actual cause was never definitely established. Marine men believe any one of these causes may have started the conflagration.

The flames fed fiercely on the freshly painted wooden superstructure of the ship and soon roared one hundred feet into the air. A second and third alarm was turned into the city fire department as the flames devoured the boat. Eleven engine companies and three hook and ladder companies were at the scene of action, and streams from fifteen hose lines deluged the fire. For three hours the firemen battled the flames before they had them under control. It was not until after two o'clock that afternoon that the fire was actually out and the apparatus ordered back to their stations.

They left behind them the most costly fire that Cleveland had experienced in many years. Firemen estimated the damage at around seven hundred thousand dollars, a part of which, the boat line officials said, was covered by insurance. A Cleveland radio station had broadcast the news of the burning vessel and thousands of fire and ship fans gathered at the scene. A major traffic jam occurred as they all converged toward the pier.

It was late into the night before the interested crowds

left the doomed and smoldering ship. The nearby *See-andbee*, moored across the slip, was towed out of danger. It was reported that the heat had blistered some of her paint before she could be moved. The *City of Erie* was moored at the bow of the *City of Buffalo* and escaped the flames.

The *City of Buffalo* had sunk at her pier, due to the immense amount of water which was poured onto the flames, and which eventually found its way into the ship's hull. The upper decks aft from amidships had collapsed and were lying in a charred mass on the main deck. Life boats were dangling crazily, some of them burned. Mattresses, chairs, tables, dishes, carpeting and the many things that go to make up a passenger steamer's equipment were all in a jumbled, blackened, sodden mass.

The *City of Buffalo* was no more. Never again would rice be thrown on her gang plank as a scurrying couple sought the shelter of her grand salon. Never again would the tired business man relax on her decks as he journeyed about, or the motorist rest in her white staterooms as he forsook the crowded highways with his car for a quiet night aboard ship. She was now ready for the salvage crew and the wrecker. Eventually she was raised and towed to a wrecker's yard and stripped to the hull. It is reported that the wreck sold to the wrecker for one thousand dollars. Her hull still floats and may some day find a useful purpose in the lake freight trade.

Thus pass the lake passenger ships of yesterday into nothing but memories. New lake passenger ships are not replacing those going into the discard and the enthusiastic lake traveler wonders what may eventually become of his summer vacation pastime. However, other ships will come to the lakes in the future, new and streamlined and swift. The public will not pass up the glories of a lake cruise so easily. They will demand new, safe, and sleek vessels and will pay well to ride on them. Other interested men will build and operate them. The call of the lakes will not be denied.

A glance into the history of the *City of Buffalo* is to go back into the days of the Gay Nineties, when lake steamer travel had growing pains. Even the *City of Buffalo* was afflicted with this malady, as, after a few years of operation, she was cut in two at a shipyard and lengthened by forty-two feet. Such was the demand for lake transportation in those days.

The *City of Buffalo* operated principally on Lake Erie on the overnight Cleveland and Buffalo run. Daylight trips were occasionally made. She early earned the title of "honeymoon special" because of the fact that she carried so many couples to that famous mecca of newlyweds, Niagara Falls, which was reached by rail or trolley and later by bus from the Buffalo dock.

The ship was built in 1896 at Wyandotte, Michigan, for the Cleveland & Buffalo Transit Company. Oddly, this concern was the only owner of the boat, as it never changed hands. In the year following her building, she came to Cleveland and, with great celebration, entered on her run. In 1898 she was joined by the *City of Erie* and the two ships made alternate trips between the two cities of Cleveland and Buffalo, occasionally going to Port Stanley on the Canadian side of Lake Erie. During the Pan-American Exposition at Buffalo in 1901 the two ships carried many thousands of people to and from the big show. The *City of Buffalo,* after her lengthening, was three hundred and fifty-six feet overall in length, and forty-three feet five inches in beam, with a depth of seventeen feet four inches.

As a boat to attract public attention the *City of Buffalo* was not very colorful. She was a dependable ship, carefully operated, and nothing of any startling nature came her way. Her nearest approach to any cause for alarm was in May, 1929. On a trip from Buffalo to Cleveland, she was caught in a howling Lake Erie gale. With her engines disabled and therefore at the mercy of wind and water for several hours, the ship was blown into the Ashtabula breakwall, causing damage to the rudder.

She carried but twenty-three passengers, as it was early in the season. These were all safely transferred in midlake to the *City of Erie* and eventually landed at Cleveland. Later, the *City of Buffalo* was towed to Cleveland and repaired, and resumed her run soon afterward.

She had a small list of captains considering the length of time that she operated. Captain John Edwards was in command of the ship when she first came out. Then followed Captain William H. Smith, a colorful character known in shipping circles as "Tiger Bill." He was fatally stricken while aboard his ship. Then came Captain A. H. MacLachlan, Captain Philip Dewan and Captain Allan Strachan. Captain John T. Eaton was her last commander. One of her last chief engineers was the late William H. Caine, who, at one time, had charge of the engine room of the luxurious lake liner *Seeandbee* belonging to the same fleet.

Note: It is possible that the stout steel hull of the old *City of Buffalo* may again sail the lakes. It was purchased by a concern operating freight ships and it is thought that the hull may be reconditioned and rebuilt into a freight carrier.

⚓ ⚓ ⚓ ⚓ ⚓ ⚓ ⚓ ⚓

Chapter Twenty

SAILOR YARNS—A STAR WHEELSMAN

Back in the old schooner days on the Great Lakes this yarn was often told.

The night was clear and the sky was bright with countless stars. The breeze was just right to send the schooner along at a brisk clip. The hands were below, asleep. Only the skipper and the wheelsman were on deck. The wheelsman was new aboard ship, having signed on that day, and knew little of what was about him.

The captain grew sleepy. He had had a busy day getting the cargo loaded and putting off to sea. He yawned a great deal. Finally Morpheus triumphed.

"Keep her Nor' Nor' West, and steady as she is, my boy, and she'll run along fine. I'm a-takin' forty winks here on this bench," said the tired skipper to the new man at the wheel as he yawned again.

"What's Nor' Nor' West, sir? Is that the way we're going now?" inquired the green man, gripping the wheel a bit firmer.

"Great Scott!" groaned the captain. "That man don't even know the compass."

Then he had an idea. Surely this would work.

"Here, look, fella. See yonder star? That bright one up there? See?" and the captain pointed upwards.

272

After some difficulty, the wheelsman said that he saw it.

"Well then, head her nose right smack at that there star, and keep her there, and you'll be all right. Forget the compass. Call me if anything goes wrong," instructed the skipper as he stretched himself full length on the bench beside the wheel.

Two hours later the captain awoke. All was just as it had been when he had dropped off to sleep, except that the schooner was considerably off her course.

"Hey, you, didn't I tell you to steer straight for that star? Now look where you got her headed," bellowed the enraged captain.

"Yes, sir, I did that, sir, and would you believe it, sir, we passed that star long ago, and I had to pick me another one," explained the would-be navigator.

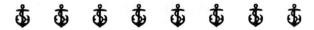

SAILOR YARNS—JINGLE BELLS

The wind was gusty and strong. It would blow first from one direction and then another. The skipper, standing on the bridge and trying to dock his long freighter, was having a tough time of it. Back a little—ahead a little—stop—ahead more—back a bit—stop, and so it went. What with the wind and the current it was devilishly difficult to put the ship on the exact spot!

His signal bells to his engineer rang sharply and almost continuously. The sweating engineer was having as hard a time of it as was the captain, perhaps harder. Stopping, starting and reversing his huge engines required much more physical labor than merely ringing an engine room telegraph.

Finally, with much ringing of bells and a great deal of shouting, coupled with considerable effective swearing, the skipper managed to get his lines ashore and made fast to the desired location. All was well now.

He came down off the bridge, paused on deck, then decided to go down to the engine room and tell the engineer what a time he had had to get her docked. Down he went. There to his astonished eyes he beheld the chief struggling with his monstrous engines, pulling this lever and that, and in general having a very tough time of it.

"Hey, what's the big idea?" called the skipper to the engineer. "We're in dock. Don't need to run the engines now. We're tied up."

"Mebbe so," replied the conscientious engineer, "but I'm just getting caught up with those signals you been a-ringin'!"

⚓ ⚓ ⚓ ⚓ ⚓ ⚓ ⚓ ⚓

SAILOR YARNS—DOLLARS TO DOUGHNUTS

A pleasing old sailor yarn is told in a recent issue of The Lake Erie Breeze, a publication of the Ashley and Dustin Steamer Line, operators of the fine day excursion steamer *Put-In-Bay* between Detroit and Sandusky.

In the sixties, seventies and well into the eighties there were more sailing boats than steam boats on the Great Lakes. It was clear sailing for the windjammers out in the lakes, but when they reached the mouth of the Detroit River sailing conditions were different. Many passenger steamers picked up considerable money on the side by towing schooners up the river to Detroit. There was a big fleet of tugs in these waters to handle this business, but nevertheless, the sidewheelers were always on the lookout for sailing vessels to tow in.

Captain Selah Dustin was running a snappy little side-wheeler between Sandusky and Detroit in those days and towed many a sailing craft into the river.

One day, in a dead calm, a schooner was laying out off Bar Point at the mouth of the Detroit River. She had no signal set for a tow, but was just riding at anchor. The steamer *Dart*, Captain Selah Dustin in command, on her way up from Put-In-Bay, pulled over to the schooner and the mate of the *Dart* threw a heaving line aboard the schooner. This was the regular way of inviting the captain of the schooner to send his tow line over to the *Dart*,

276

but the captain of the schooner threw the line off his deck.

The captain of the *Dart* was not to be put off so easily and began to bargain with the schooner people.

"This dead calm may last for a week," roared Captain Dustin, "and there's no telling when you will reach Detroit; I'll tow you in for twenty-five dollars."

"Not this ship," roared back the captain of the schooner, "I've got plenty of time to wait for a breeze; family is all on board; plenty of grub and tobacco; and my wife is a good cook."

Just then the tantalizing aroma of hot cooking was wafted aboard the sidewheeler and Captain Dustin, with his mouth watering, said, "Maybe you are frying doughnuts? They sure do smell good."

Captain Dustin weakened as the delicious aroma of the fried cakes sailed over from the schooner's galley, and finally, he called over, "I'll tell you what I'll do, captain. Just send me over a mess of those doughnuts and I'll tow you up for ten dollars."

The doughnuts and the schooner's tow line came over without further delay.

♧ ♧ ♧ ♧ ♧ ♧ ♧ ♧

SAILOR YARNS—COLD LYING

Thirty degrees below zero is pretty cold. For many long hours the crew had battled to put their freighter into port at Fort William, the Canadian head of the Great Lakes, and there to tie up for the winter. If they were able to reach dock before dark they might get back to their homes by Christmas. But it was tough going. Ice was forming fast, and it was all the ship could do to force its way through. Several times it looked as though the ice would close in on the vessel and lock it fast until spring.

At last they made the harbor and the skipper donned all his togs, and some of the mate's, and went out on the icy bridge in the sub-zero twilight to supervise the docking of his ship. He directed that the vessel be tied up at the nearest available dock.

The ship had just been placed exactly on the spot that the captain wanted and the lines were just being made fast, when an hysterical irate individual came running and shouting down the dock, waving his arms wildly. He galloped to the bow and looked up to where the captain stood on the bridge, high as a six-story building.

"Hey, you can't dock here," he bellowed to the skipper. "You'll hafta get out of here! This is a private dock. Get out!"

He waved his arms and shook his fists frantically.

SAILOR YARNS

The weary skipper was thinking fast. Just a few more minutes was all that he needed. Nature would take care of the rest. He cupped his hand behind his muffled ear.

"Can't hear a thing you say," he shouted down to the wildly gesticulating man on the dock, and lying like the good sailor that he was, added, "Wait a few minutes and I'll come down and see you."

"Get out of here! Get this boat away from here! Can you hear that?" he bawled at the skipper.

"I still can't hear you," roared back the old man from his lofty bridge.

He crossed over to the opposite side of the ship and looked down at the rapidly freezing water. Already the vessel was gripped fast in the ice. They were safe there until spring. Nothing short of dynamite could move the ship now.

"Guess it'll be all right now to go down and see that feller," he remarked to the frozen atmosphere. "We're in afore dark and snugly berthed for the winter. Owners'll pay him well for his dockage. Ho, hum, it's sure a-freezin' fast."

⚓ ⚓ ⚓ ⚓ ⚓ ⚓ ⚓ ⚓

SAILOR YARNS—WHISTLE AWAY

Like most of the sailor yarns in this book, this one is claimed to be based on the truth. It has to do with the advent of the steam whistle, that indispensible mariners' aid. It would be impossible now to safely navigate the waters of the Great Lakes without the whistle. It is the first thought of the men in charge of ships when danger threatens. Even the lowly row boat equipped with an outboard motor is required by law to carry a whistle, albeit, blown by the lung power of the boatman. The tale of the first Great Lakes whistle follows.

William McGee, fiery Irishman and chief engineer of the old steamboat *Rochester,* was outfitting and overhauling his ship during the winter of 1843-44, in the harbor of Buffalo. He had run across a description and plans of a crude steam whistle in a foreign paper and was experimenting with the contraption during the overhauling of the *Rochester.* The result of his labors brought forth the first steam whistle.

It produced an ear-splitting terrorizing blast that frightened all who were unfortunate enough to be within sound of it. It was installed on the *Rochester* when she sailed the following spring, more for the novelty of the thing than for any practical reason.

Engineer McGee numbered among his enemies one Captain Charles L. Gager, master of the steamer *General Porter.* On her first trip up the lakes that season the

Rochester overtook the *General Porter* near Bois Blanc Light in the Straits of Mackinac. She ran alongside the *General Porter*. McGee was ready with his whistle. The fun loving engineer let go with a blood-curdling blast on his new contraption. He blew it long and loud. It startled Captain Gager and his good crew almost out of their senses.

The *Rochester* then pulled ahead of the *General Porter* and docked at Mackinac. Meantime the *General Porter* followed along the same route. Her captain was furious at the "insult" to himself, his ship and her crew. He vowed dire vengeance when next he saw the *Rochester*. His chance came when he reached Mackinac for, when he arrived there, he found the object of his wrath tied to a dock.

Upon docking his ship, Captain Gager hurried over to the *Rochester* and, unaware that his arch enemy, McGee, was the man who had given him the "raspberries," he shouted from the dock for the man to come forward that had made such a squawk at him. McGee hopped to the dock obligingly. Loud and harsh words filled the quiet air. Fists started flying. Bystanders halted the fracas.

McGee's steam whistle soon became an object of interest to shipowners and operators. In place of it being a mere novelty, it became a useful adjunct to the vesselmen. It soon replaced the old time bell and cannon. Ashore, factories found it useful. The whistle, born in strife, was here to stay.

⚓ ⚓ ⚓ ⚓ ⚓ ⚓ ⚓ ⚓

SAILOR YARNS—AS THE BOOK SAYETH

Daylight was just breaking over the water after a wild and stormy night. The lighthouse keeper climbed the long flight of spiral stairs and extinguished the light and hung its cloth covering around it to protect it from the bright sun's rays that might soon peep out of the east.

He looked far below at the troubled waters. Huge waves broke and roared upon the shore. White water tumbled about as far as his eye could see.

What was that fleck of a different white out yonder? The grizzled lighthouse keeper grabbed for his binoculars, adjusted them to his eyes, located the white fleck. It floated sluggishly in the water.

"Great Caesar!" groaned the keeper. "It's a small gasoline cruiser and he's tied his shirt on his flag mast. It's a wonder he floats at all in that sea. Distress call, sure enough."

Down those long stairs the keeper went, straight to his surf boat. He hurried to launch it into the heaving seas. He shouted for his assistant, who presently appeared and lent the old man a hand.

The distressed cruiser had also been sighted by a passing truck driver, off to an early morning start along the road at the top of the bluff. He had turned off the highway and was coming down the little side road to the lighthouse. He left his truck and came to where the men were launching their small boat.

"Hey, you fellows, see that cruiser out there?" he shouted above the noise of the breakers.

The two workers nodded silently.

"You're not a-goin' out there to it in that there little tub, are ya?" he asked in amazement, and continued helpfully, "you'll never get back if you do!"

"Mister," said the old keeper, turning to the stranger, "our book here says that we gotta go out; it doesn't say we gotta come back!"

⚓ ⚓ ⚓ ⚓ ⚓ ⚓ ⚓ ⚓

SAILOR YARNS—SCOTTY'S BOOKKEEPING

A recent issue of the Lake Erie Breeze, published by Ashley and Dustin Line, Detroit, tells this one.

Scotty Blake was an old-time steamboat fireman. He had a steady job aboard the steamer *Frank E. Kirby,* which years ago sailed from Detroit. His credit was good at Baltimore Red's.

Scotty, taking his regular drink, sometimes a bit more, paid Baltimore Red every pay day. Scotty, however, had a growing suspicion that he was paying for more drinks than he consumed. In order to keep tab himself, Scotty would take a coffee bean from the "breath dish" on the end of the bar and put it in his pocket. When he settled with Red, he would count the beans, at a bean a drink, and so check pretty closely with Red's books.

This bright idea worked fine until Connie, the dock boss, got next to Scotty's tactics and decided to do something about it. One evening in the fall, right at pay day, all was merry at Red's and a goodly crowd of sailors was there. Connie worked in close to Scotty and slipped a handful of the coffee beans into that unsuspecting individual's pocket.

Well, when Scotty came to check up, he protested before he even saw the bill. That night Scotty changed boats and shipped north on a lumber hooker and remained in the lumber camps all winter.

284

⚓ ⚓ ⚓ ⚓ ⚓ ⚓ ⚓ ⚓

SAILOR YARNS—MIGHT AIN'T RIGHT

Another good lake yarn is related in the Lake Erie Breeze. It follows.

When the Michigan lumber camps were thriving in the eighties, the big lumber companies had their own fleet of lumber boats and, on the up trips, would take on supplies at Detroit.

This made big business for the docks. When loading freight it was the mate's job to see that the ship got all that the shipping bills called for, and this was a big job when they had to look out for breakages as well. The boats would dock at all hours. Some of these mates were pretty tough boys, but many of them have turned out to be big passenger captains, in full regalia and very polite to the ladies. The brothers Gallagher were rough, and could they cuss? Nothing could be put over on those boys—much.

It took Connie, the kidder, and boss of the dock, to show them up finally. On this particular occasion, a raw night in November, with a warehouse full of freight and everybody disagreeable, the Gallaghers were watching every bag, box and barrel that was being loaded. Now, a box of lamp chimneys generally rattles, but the box in question rattled more than usual and Connie was watching his chance to get it on the boat and thus out of his care. He finally loaded it on a stevedore's truck and the box got about half way to the gang-plank when one of the Gallaghers heard the jingling and he let out a roar.

"Hey, you, what the hell you giving me there?"

Connie replied, "Sleighbells."

"All right," said Gallagher.

Some of the boys are laughing yet.

⚓ ⚓ ⚓ ⚓ ⚓ ⚓ ⚓ ⚓

SAILOR YARNS—THAT JUG OF WINE

Cut rates and price wars raged in the old days, even as they do today. Along in the 1840's more ships were in the lakes' trade than the amount of business warranted. The old economic law of "supply and demand" quickly brought about drastic cuts in rates among these ships and passengers were often hauled free of charge just to beat a rival line. The story of a captain whose ship lay at a dock in Buffalo awaiting passengers in those times is interesting.

The captain was approached by a traveler and asked what his cabin rates were to Detroit. The captain, anxious for the business, promptly quoted a rate that was about one-half his regular one. The traveler was invited aboard the ship to look her over, and free drinks were served as an extra inducement.

The traveler, however, decided to shop further. Later he was found by the captain and was asked what he had decided. The crafty traveler informed the skipper that he had found another ship that would carry him free.

"Well, in that case," said the captain, "I'll do the same, and besides that I'll give you all your meals also."

"No, I don't think I'll ride with you," replied the shopper. "You see, I believe I like his wine better than yours!"

⚓ ⚓ ⚓ ⚓ ⚓ ⚓ ⚓ ⚓

SAILOR YARNS—LAND LUBBER LADY

Probably the most up-to-the-minute yarn is the one about the skipper whose ship had just been equipped with the new radio telephone ship-to-shore apparatus. The ship was banging through a stiff wind, upbound, on Lake Huron. Early in the evening the captain decided to try the new contrivance by putting in a call to his wife.

The call was put through promptly and the skipper heard the shrill voice of his wife's sister on the land end of the connection.

"That you, Tillie?" he shouted.

"Sure, it's me. Who'd you suppose it was? Mary's gone to the movies, and I came over to stay with the kids until she gets back," came the reply. Then she added, "What are you shouting so for, Jack? A person would think that you never used a phone before."

"Well, I never did, not just like this," he went on to explain. "This one's on the ship, and we're out in Lake Huron."

"Land sakes, Jack! How you can think up the darndest jokes!" the good land-lubber lady remarked.

The conversation ended shortly. When Mary returned, her ever suspicious sister, innocent of marine affairs, informed her that Jack had phoned and that she was certain he had been drinking a bit too much.

SAILOR YARNS

"He said he was out in Lake Huron and that it was rough, and that the waves were banging against the ship. Seems to me if them wires out there was a-risin' and a-fallin' on the waves I'd of heard it on the telephone," the good sister remarked dryly.

⚓ ⚓ ⚓ ⚓ ⚓ ⚓ ⚓ ⚓

SAILOR YARNS—LOOK OUT

The night was dark. The freighter plowed her way through the blackness. The captain was in the pilot house with the helmsman. The lookout was stationed at his post in the extreme bow of the ship.

Suddenly the men in the pilot house saw another ship bearing down on them. Quickly the captain ordered the ship turned to avoid a collision, just in the nick of time. The two vessels slid past each other with little to spare.

The lookout in the bow had said never a word. The skipper was furious.

"Did you see that ship a-coming?" he bawled at the lookout.

"Sure, I saw it," replied that young man smartly, "didn't you?"

"You should have reported seeing it, just as soon as you first spied it. That's your duty," admonished the old skipper, disgustedly.

"Oh yeah," replied the smart lookout. "Maybe I coulda seen it sooner if I'da climbed out on that there steering pole. Want me to try it next time?"

The hardened old captain felt his hand closing into a big horny fist, but he turned away from his fresh lookout and mumbled something terrible in his beard as he returned to the pilot house.

The young lookout was fired at the next port. Time

went on. A year passed and he was still without work. He decided to write the old skipper for his job back. But the captain wasn't a man to forget or forgive. He smiled as he read the letter from his snippy former lookout, and he sat down and scrawled across the bottom of the letter, "Why don't you climb out on a steering pole somewhere and see if you can't see a job?"

⚓ ⚓ ⚓ ⚓ ⚓ ⚓ ⚓ ⚓

SAILOR YARNS—HASTE AND WASTE

This yarn is told with a chuckle by an old mate on a lake passenger ship.

A taxi rushed down to the dock and came to a quick stop with a great howling of brakes and scraping of tires. A nervous little man with a large suitcase popped out.

"I'll make it all right," he shouted over his shoulder to the driver, as he rushed pell-mell to the water's edge. The ship was now two feet from the dock.

With his hat pulled down tight over his head and clutching fast to his suitcase, the man pushed aside the restraining hands of the men on the dock and made a flying leap to the deck of the ship. He was caught by the mate as he skidded aboard.

"Gosh! That was close. I almost missed the boat," said the man, all out of breath, "but I made it!"

"You sure did, mister," answered the ship's officer. "But what's your hurry? Why the hell don't you wait until we can get the boat up to the dock?"

⚓ ⚓ ⚓ ⚓ ⚓ ⚓ ⚓ ⚓

SAILOR YARNS—SEA-GOING PHARMACY

Many stories are told of the shortcomings of the lookout, that safety man of the crew, who stands his lonely watch in the bow of his ship, and when any activity is sighted he reports it to the navigating officer.

An Irishman was given the job of lookout on an early steamer of the Great Lakes. Ever watchful and mindful of his instructions, the new lookout hailed the bridge on his first night on duty.

"I see something straight ahead, sor," he reported.

"What do ya see?" roared back the officer.

"Begorra, sor, I don't know what I see. It has red and green lights. Sure now, and maybe it's a drug store!"

⚓ ⚓ ⚓ ⚓ ⚓ ⚓ ⚓ ⚓

SAILOR YARNS—A LARGE PARTY

Half a century ago a dozen or so warehousemen and stevedores sat on a dock in Detroit awaiting the arrival of a steamer.

Many and varied were the topics of their conversation. In some manner Pontius Pilate came up for discussion. The deep throated sound of the incoming ship's whistle interrupted their talk and the men strolled over to the dock's edge to watch the steamer tie up.

The captain was at his post on the vessel's bridge, directing the docking. He was a very large man with a tremendous paunch.

The local wit saw his chance and shouted, "Look, fellows, there he is in the flesh, old Paunch-us Pilot himself."

⚓ ⚓ ⚓ ⚓ ⚓ ⚓ ⚓ ⚓

SAILOR YARNS—THE FOLLOW-UP SYSTEM

Lake navigation today is a systematic business. Definite schedules of the freighters are maintained, and the dispatchers in the home office of any fleet can spot where their ships are on the chart at any moment. Aboard ship the masters know almost where they are in their sleep. But this is today. Years ago things were not so definite.

Captain Bluff sailed the lakes years ago. Some of the old-timers still recall his type. He was a gruff old guy with a bellowing fearsome voice, a huge frame, big fists and a canny brain. How he ever managed to obtain his papers to navigate a ship was never clearly understood by outsiders. But he had them, and he managed to get a freighter to command.

He was always most careful about picking his mate. Captain Bluff always made certain that his mate knew navigation. If there was any doubt about the matter old Bluff looked farther. He also liked a mate that didn't require much sleep, and one that he could browbeat.

One foggy evening found Captain Bluff's ship passing Port Huron, up bound, and entering big Lake Huron. They had followed another freighter up the St. Clair River leading to the lake.

"I'm sick, cap'n," said the luckless mate to Bluff, just at this point. "I gotta go lay me down. Can't stand up no longer."

"Wattsa matter with ya?" growled the captain. "Ye ain't gettin' delicate, are ya?"

He glanced ahead at the freighter they were following and grinned to himself.

"All right, go lay down; I'll carry on," Bluff told his mate.

The mate went below.

"What course now, sir?" inquired the wheelsman of Captain Bluff when they were alone in the pilot house.

Captain Bluff really didn't know, now that his mate was not on deck, but he was prepared.

"Might as well just follow that boat ahead. That'll save us setting a course. We'll let him do that work. Fog's not so thick but what you can see his lights. Keep your peepers on him and don't lose him, and he'll show us the way to Duluth without no trouble."

"Yes, sir," said the wheelsman.

Captain Bluff dozed in the quiet comfort of the pilot house. The fog lifted and his wheelsman could follow the ship ahead without difficulty.

So on through the night went the ship under the command of Captain Bluff.

Then came the dawn. They were still a respectable distance astern of the leading ship. But land was appearing on their bows where ordinarily no land should be. Something was definitely wrong. The wheelsman awakened his captain.

"Somethin' wrong, sir. I ain't never saw no land off'n there before, not so soon anyhow," complained the puzzled man at the wheel, and continued, "I been a-followin' that there boat ahead all night, and there she still is."

"Great Caesar, sumpin's sure wrong! Call the mate, sick or no, fetch him here. Quick, I'll steer," cried the follow-up captain.

Presently the mate appeared in the pilot house doorway.

"Hey, where in hell are we?" roared the captain to his mate.

"Looks sorta like Goderich to me," replied the mate. "Yes, sir, by gosh! That's what she is, sure 'nuff, Goderich."

"Goderich!" shouted Captain Bluff. "Hell's bells! What's that feller ahead a-goin' to Goderich for? Ain't never had this happen a-fore. Turn us about and set course for Duluth, quick. Six hours lost already. Hurry now, and look sharp. Ring the engine room for more speed, we gotta make time now."

The ship swung her prow outward into the lake toward the Duluth course as the mate and the wheelsman compared notes.

"Won't say it's any of my mistake," Bluff said to himself.

He turned to the mate and said, "You take over now, mister. I guess you can stand it. I'm goin' below and get me some rest."

"Yes, sir," replied the mate, as he winked at the wheelsman.

"I'll wire the office that we wuz hung up in the fog last night, soon as we get to the Soo. They'll never know the difference," remarked Bluff to himself and the old scoundrel pulled up the covers and slept soundly knowing the mate was on watch.

⚓ ⚓ ⚓ ⚓ ⚓ ⚓ ⚓ ⚓

SAILOR YARNS—PAPER LOSSES

Here is a true yarn, told by a shipowner on himself. We'll call his vessel the *Lumber King,* which, of course, is not its real name, but a good one for our purpose.

The *Lumber King* had outlived her (or his) usefulness, at least until more money would be spent on it to repair this and that. But, one day along came a man who wanted to buy her, for purposes of his own, and at a handsome profit to the present owner. Would the owner fix her up and sell her? He most certainly would!

Further negotiations were carried on by mail for a long time, (the prospective purchaser living in another lake city), but finally the deal fell through. The owner was thoroughly discouraged. He shortly ordered the old *Lumber King* dismantled. The wreckers attacked the ship with a will and commenced cutting up the boilers and engines in high glee.

For three days they labored, and felt they had done a good job. Parts, very vital parts, of the old ship, were all cut up and lying about the dock. A real wrecker enjoys nothing better than wrecking.

On the fourth day the discouraged owner arrived at his desk. On it lay a telegram from his former prospect. It informed him that that individual was on his way to buy the ship, for cash, and was bringing the check to cover in full with him.

298

The distraught owner hurried over to the dock to look over the dismembered *Lumber King*. Alas! Too late! The wreckers had done their work too well. The ship was now beyond redemption. He thought of that check the would-be buyer had in his pocket for him. He became ill as he looked woefully at the wreckage strewn about him. He returned sadly to his office.

The would-be buyer was there waiting. The owner mournfully explained what had happened. Too late! Just four days too late!

Then it was the buyer's turn to feel ill. He moaned.

"And to think that I had that ship sold to another fellow for twice what I was to pay you for it," he groaned.

"Too late!" sighed the owner.

"Too bad!" sighed the buyer. He tore the check in tiny pieces and tossed them ruefully into the wastebasket.

⚓ ⚓ ⚓ ⚓ ⚓ ⚓ ⚓ ⚓

SAILOR YARNS—NAUTICAL CHOP-STIX

A lake captain who was asked by his wife to look at some pianos while in Detroit, with a view of buying one for her, wrote home to her the following letter:

"Dear Millie:

"I saw a piano that I believe will suit you; black walnut hull, strong bulkheads, strengthened fore and aft with iron frame, ceiled with whitewood and maple. Rigging steel wire and double on the ratlines and whipped wire on the lower stays, and heavier cordage. Belaying pins of steel and well driven home. Length of taffrail over all, 6 feet 2 inches. This light draft makes the craft equally serviceable in high seas or low flats. It has two martingales, one for the light airs and zephyr winds and one for strong gusts and sudden squalls. Both are worked with foot rests, near the keelson, handy for the quartermaster and out o' sight of the passengers. The running gear from the hand rail to the cordage is made of whitewood and holly; works free and clear; strong enough for the requirements of a musical tornado, and gentle enough for the requiem of a departing class. Hatches, black walnut; can be battened down proof against ten-year-old boys and commercial drummers, or can be clewed up, on occasion, and sheeted home for a first class instrumental cyclone. I sailed the craft a little, and thought she had a list to starboard. Anyhow, I liked the starboard side better than the port, but the shipkeeper told me that the owner had other craft of like tonnage awaiting sale or charter, which were on just even keel.

"Yours,"

"Jack."

From The Lake Erie Breeze.

⚓ ⚓ ⚓ ⚓ ⚓ ⚓ ⚓ ⚓

CHAPTER TWENTY-ONE

MAJOR DISASTERS OF THE GREAT LAKES

June 16, 1834—Steamer *Washington* burned on her maiden voyage in Lake Erie, off Dunkirk, N. Y.— 30 dead.

August 9, 1841—Steamer *Erie* burned in Lake Erie, off Silver Creek, N. Y.—175 dead.

Nov. 21, 1847—Steamer *Phoenix* burned in Lake Michigan, between Manitowoc and Sheboygan, Wis.—247 dead.

June 18, 1850—Steamer *G. P. Griffin* burned in Lake Erie, near Willoughby, Ohio—94 dead.

August 30, 1852—Steamer *Atlantic* sank after collision with steamer *Ogdensburgh*, in Lake Erie, near Long Point, Ontario—250 dead.

. . . . 1857—Steamer *Montreal* burned in the St. Lawrence River, two miles off Lake Ontario—250 dead.

Sept. 8, 1860—Excursion steamer *Lady Elgin* sank in Lake Michigan, between Chicago and Milwaukee, in a gale, after being rammed by the schooner *Augusta* —287 dead.

Same year in November the steamer *Dacotah* foundered in Lake Erie; all hands lost.

June 21, 1868—Passenger steamer *Morning Star* sank in Lake Erie, off Lorain, Ohio, after collision with the schooner *Courtland*—23 dead.

Same year the steamer *Seabird* burned in Lake Michigan—100 dead.

302

MAJOR DISASTERS OF THE LAKES

Jan. 21, 1895—Steamer *Chicora* sank in Lake Michigan —26 dead.

Nov. 30, 1905—Steamer *Mataafa* ashore at Duluth, Minn.—9 dead. Later salvaged and returned to service.

.... 1908—Steamer *D. M. Clemson* sank in Lake Superior—24 dead.

.... 1909—Steamer *Russia* foundered in Lake Huron— 13 dead.

Same year, steamer *Tempest No. 2* burned in Georgian Bay—6 dead.

Same year, steamer *Badger State* burned in Lake Huron—15 dead.

Same year, steamer *Clarion* burned in Lake Erie—32 dead.

Same year, carferry *Marquette & Bessemer No. 2* disappeared between Conneaut, Ohio, and Port Stanley, Ontario, in Lake Erie—36 lost.

.... 1911—Tug *Silver Spray* sank off Cleveland—9 dead.

Nov. 11, 1913—The "Big Storm." Steamers lost were: *Argus; James Carruthers; Hydrus; Leafield; John A. McGean; Charles S. Price; Regina; Isaac M. Scott; Henry B. Smith; Wexford* and *Lightship No. 82.* Several others driven ashore, badly damaged. Total dead estimated at 244.

Same year on Nov. 26th, the schooner *Rouse Simmons* foundered in Lake Michigan, off Kewaunee, Wis.—17 dead.

Nov. 19, 1914—Steamer *C. F. Curtis* with barges *Marvin* and *Peterson* in tow disappeared near Grand Marais, Mich.—26 lost.

July 24, 1915—The greatest single tragedy of the lakes, the excursion steamer *Eastland* overturned in the Chicago River—835 dead.

.... 1915—Tug *Frank C. Barnes* and sandsucker *Junior* sank—11 lost.

Oct. 20, 1916—"Black Friday." Steamers *James B. Colgate; Merida* and schooner *D. L. Filer*, all foundered in Lake Erie—49 lost. Steamer *Marshall F. Butters* sank in Lake Erie but her crew were rescued.

Nov. 24, 1918—Two new mine sweepers built for France, the *Cerisoler* and the *Inkerman*, disappeared in Lake Superior on maiden voyage from Fort William to Kingston, Ontario, enroute to France. No trace of them ever found—76 lost.

.... 1919—Steamers *Myron; H. E. Runnels* and *John Owen*, sank in gale in upper lakes; approximately 40 lost.

Aug. 20, 1920—Steamer *Superior City* sank in Lake Superior in a collision with steamer *Willis L. King*—29 dead.

Dec. 21, 1922—Tug *Cornell* lost in Lake Erie—8 dead.

Sept. 22, 1924—Whaleback steamer *Clifton* sank in Lake Huron—28 lost.
Same year, wooden steamer *Orinoco* sank in Lake Huron—4 lost.

.... 1925—Sandsucker *Kelley Island* sank in Lake Erie —9 dead. Later salvaged and returned to service.

Dec. 6, 1927—Steamer *Kamloops* disappeared in Lake Superior—22 lost.

MAJOR DISASTERS OF THE LAKES

Oct. 22, 1929—Carferry *Milwaukee* sank in Lake Michigan, out of Milwaukee—52 lost.
Later that year the steamer *Wisconsin* sank near the same spot—16 dead.
Same year the steamer *Chicago* went aground on Michipicoten Island in Lake Superior; crew rescued.
Same year gravel carrier *Andaste* foundered in Lake Michigan—25 dead.

July 29, 1930—Steamer *George J. Whelan* foundered in Lake Erie, off Dunkirk—15 dead.

Oct. 5, 1932—Steamer *John J. Boland, Jr.,* foundered in Lake Erie, off Barcelona, N. Y.—4 dead.

July 27, 1936—Sandsucker *Material Service* sank off Chicago—15 dead.

Oct. 17, 1936—Sandsucker *Sand Merchant* foundered in Lake Erie, off Cleveland—19 dead.

May 1, 1940—Steamer *Arlington* sank in Lake Superior—1 dead.

June, 1940—Wooden steamer *Sidney O. Neff* sank at Menominee Harbor, Mich. One of the last wooden ships of the lakes. No lives lost.

TABLE OF SAILING DISTANCES ON THE
GREAT LAKES

Between	Buffalo	Cleveland	Detroit	Mackinac Island	Saulte Ste. Marie	Houghton
Duluth	1,115	935	830	525	420	180
Cleveland	180					
Detroit	285	105				
Mackinac Island	590	410	305			
Saulte Ste. Marie	695	515	410	105		
Houghton	935	755	650	345	240	
Milwaukee	866	686	581	276	Milwaukee	
Chicago	951	771	666	361	85	

LORE OF THE LAKES

TABLE OF SAILING TIME BETWEEN
PRINCIPAL LAKE PORTS

Based on average speed of 11 to 12 miles per hour.

Approximate
Hours Required

Duluth to Sault Ste. Marie 36

Sault Ste. Marie to Detour 5

Detour to Port Huron 20

Port Huron to Livingstone Channel 7½

Livingstone Channel to Cleveland 9

Livingstone Channel to Buffalo 24

Livingstone Channel to Erie 17

Detour to Mackinac Island 4

Mackinac Island to Indiana Harbor or
   South Chicago 32

Vessels without cargo will make slightly better time than shown above.

SCALE OF STATUTE AND NAUTICAL MILES

The Statute Mile is 5,280 feet.
The British Knot or Nautical Mile is 6,080 feet.
The Statute Knot is 6,082.66 feet.

1 knot equals 1.151 miles	5 knots equal 5.757 miles
2 knots equal 2.303 miles	10 knots equal 11.515 miles
3 knots equal 3.454 miles	20 knots equal 23.030 miles
4 knots equal 4.606 miles	25 knots equal 28.787 miles

6 feet equal 1 fathom
600 feet equal 1 cable
10 cables equal 1 knot

ROMAN NOTATION

I	1	VI	6	XI	11
II	2	VII	7	XII	12
III	3	VIII	8	XIII	13
IV	4	IX	9	XIV	14
V	5	X	10	XV	15

XVI	16	XXX	30	LXXX or	
XVII	17	XL	40	XXC	80
XVIII	18	L	50	XC	90
XIX	19	LX	60	C	100
XX	20	LXX	70	CC	200

CCC	300	DCCC	800
CCCC	400	CM	900
D	500	M or cIc	1000
DC	600	MM	2000
DCC	700	MMM	3000

INDEX OF SHIPS

Abyssinia 103*, 237
Acadian 192
Accommodation 7, 42
Alabama..............139*, 12, 77, 78, 250
Alaska 72
Algomah 16
Algomah II 249
Alpena 168
Andaste 21, 305
Andrews, Mathew 192
Argus..............127*, 19, 194, 303
Ariel 37
Arlington 22, 305
Arrow..............114*, 115*, 73, 74, 75
Assiniboia 254
Astor, J. J...............9
Atlantic 12, 302
Augusta 13, 302

Badger State 19, 303
Bainbridge 77
Baltimore 78
Bannockburn 111*, 168
Barnes 304
Barnum, G. G...............194
Bennington, U. S. S...............162
Billings, Frank R...............214, 215
Block, L. E...............223, 231
Block, Philip D...............238
Boeckling, G. A...............244
Boland, Jr., John J...............22, 305
Bradley, Carl D. 143*, 223, 229
Briton 217
Burger 170
Butler, Jr., Joseph G...............237
Butters, Marshall F...............
..............102*, 20, 214, 215, 304

Cadillac 74
Caledonia 37
Candiana 247
Carolina 77
Carruthers, James ....
..............122*, 19, 192, 194, 195, 303
Case, J. I...............15
Cerisoler 20, 169, 304
Champion 235
Chandler, Zak 96*
Chicago 21, 305
Chicora 17, 167, 303
China 100*, 15, 64, 65

Chippewa, sail 38
Chippewa, stmr. 132*, 74, 75, 80
City of Alpena 73, 79
City of Benton Harbor 77
City of Buffalo 131*, 13, 17
..............22, 62, 75, 187, 266 to 270
City of Cheboygan 249, 250
City of Cleveland II 16, 78
City of Cleveland III 141*, 79, 252
City of Detroit 15, 78
City of Detroit II..............16, 75, 79
City of Detroit III..............137*, 79, 252
City of Erie....117*, 17, 18, 73, 74,
76, 116, 180 to 187, 266, 268 to 270
City of Flint No. 32..............248
City of Glasgow 103*, 237
City of Grand Rapids 77, 247
City of Hancock 75, 244
City of Holland 77
City of Mackinac 16, 73, 78, 79
City of Midland 147*
City of Munising..............248 to 250
City of Saginaw No. 31 248
City of Saugatuck 77
City of Savannah 8, 43
City of St. Ignace 79
City of St. Joseph 77
City of The Straits 79
City of Toledo 72, 73
Clarion 19, 303
Clay, Henry 8
Clemson, D. M...............18, 303
Clermont 7, 42
Clevelander 142*
Clifton..............21, 174 to 176, 235, 304
Clint, C. K...............88*, 235
Colgate, James B...............
..............112*, 20, 209 to 213, 304
Collingwood 22
Colonel 179
Columbia 73, 246
Columbus, Christopher ....
..............104*, 17, 76, 77, 234
Cornell 20, 169, 304
Coulby, Harry ....
..............146*, 21, 223, 227, 228, 231
Courtland 14, 302
Crescent City 12, 62
Curtis, C. F...............
..............99*, 19, 172 to 174, 303

Note: * Indicates illustration.

311

Dacotah 302
Dart 72, 276, 277
Davis, Lyman M...............................15
Detroit 7, 38
Dinkey, Alva C..............................110*
Dolphin 11
Dows, David 16
Dutch Boy 170

Eastern States 79, 252
Eastland ....
..........108* 110*, 20, 201 to 208, 304
Empire 11
Empire State 60
Erie 10, 302
Erie Isles 244
Eureka 12, 60

Farrell, James A.............................133*
Fessendon, Wm. A........................ 74
Filer, D. L....................20, 215, 304
Forest City 78
Frontenac 8, 9, 42
Fulton, Robert 192

Garretson, General 121*
Georgian 251
Gillies, Donald B...........................237
Glencairn 174, 175, 176
Goodtime 75, 76, 80
Grammer, G. J...............................193
Great Western 10, 43
Greater Buffalo ....
..............140*, 79, 251, 252, 257, 258
Greater Detroit ....
..............140*, 79, 251, 252, 257, 258
Greyhound 72, 73
Griffin ....82*, 6, 31 to 34
Griffin, G. P....................12, 302
Griffon, see Griffin

Hackett, R. J.................................... 14
Hadley, George 18
Halstead 193
Hamonic 253
Hanna, Jr., Howard M.......................
..........................19, 192, 194, 199
Hardwick 193
Harlem 97*
Hartwell, Fred G.......192, 199, 214, 215
Hawgood, H. B..............................193
Hayes, R. B..................................114*

Hoyt, James H................................ 18
Hulst, John...................22, 223, 228
Hunter, General 38
Huron, schooner 6
Huron, stmr. 76
Huronic 192
Hutchinson, Charles L..................133*
Hutchinson, John T..........................193
Hutt, Hattie 90*
Hydrus................123*, 19, 194, 195, 303

Idlewild 73
Illinois 10
India...................100*, 101*, 15, 64, 65
Inkerman 20, 169, 304
Irvin, Wm. A....................22, 228
Island Queen 98*, 53

Japan 100*, 15, 64, 65
Jenks, J. M...................................192
Johnson, C. H................................96*
Joy, James F.................................. 16
Juniata...........119*, 18, 22, 65, 66, 80
Junior 304

Kamloops...........128*, 21, 176, 177, 304
Keewatin 254
Kelley Island 21, 304
Kerr, D. G....................221, 222
King, Willis L. 227, 304
Kirby, Frank E................................
...................118*, 72, 73, 74, 181, 284

Lady Elgin 13, 302
Lady Prevost 38
La Fayette 194
Lakeland 198
La Petite 235
La Salle 74
Lawrence......................83*, 36, 37
Leafield.........123*, 19, 193 to 195, 303
Le Griffon, see Griffin
Lemoyne 145*, 230
Lightship No. 61...........................193
Lightship No. 82..............................
..........................19, 193, 194, 199, 303
Little Belt 38
Louisiana 193
Lusitania 20

Mackinac, U. S. S...........................174
Mackinac Islander 249

Note: * Indicates illustration.

Mackinaw City 249
Major 194
Manitoba 254
Maplecourt 70, 80
Marquette & Bessemer No. 1........165
Marquette & Bessemer No. 2........
............................19, 168, 213, 303
Marvin, Seldon E.....19, 172 to 174, 303
Mataafa 18, 303
Material Service 22, 305
Mather, Samuel, former........175, 235
Matoa 192
Mayflower 5
May Queen 78
McGean, John A............................
............................124*, 19, 194, 195, 238, 303
Merchant 14, 15, 223, 225
Merida 20, 217, 304
Meteor 14
Michigan, schooner 6
Michigan 9
Michigan, U. S. S............................
............................94*, 11, 12, 49 to 55, 64
Midland City 254
Miller, Governor........144*, 22, 223, 228
Mills, D. O. 193
Milwaukee, early 225
Milwaukee........21, 177, 178, 179, 305
Mississippi 12, 62, 63
Missouri 78
Montauk 255
Montreal 13, 302
Morning Star 14, 78, 302
Morrell, D. J............................ 18
Morrill 217
Morro Castle 22, 66
Mullen, Martin 237
Myron 20, 304

Nancy 7
Neff, Sidney O............................305
Nelson, Wm. 87
Newark, U. S. S............................162
Niagara ....
............................83*, 84*, 85*, 35 to 41, 49, 55
Nina ....161 to 164
Noronic 139*, 253
North American 250
Northern Indiana 13, 61
Northern Queen 193
North Land............17, 20, 67 to 69, 71
North Lake 120*

North Star 14
North West, early............................ 78
North West ....
............106*, 107*, 17, 19, 67 to 70, 80
Nottingham, Wm.......19, 192, 194, 198

Octorara..........119*, 19, 22, 65, 66, 80
Ogdensburgh 12, 302
Onoko............98*, 16, 20, 223, 225, 226
Ontario 8, 9, 42
Orinoco 101*, 21, 304
Osceola 10
Oswego 11
Otter 6
Our Son 87*
Owana 72
Owen, John 20, 238, 304

Pacific 11
Paine, Wm. A............................130*, 237
Palmer, Julia 11
Pamlico 15
Parsons, Philo 53
Pere Marquette Nos. 12, 14, 17, 18,
19, 21, 22............................248
Pere Marquette No. 20............248, 250
Peterson, Annie M............................
............................19, 172 to 174, 303
Pewabic 14
Phoenix 12, 302
Pinta ....161 to 164
Plymouth, barge 193, 200
Plymouth Rock 12, 62, 63
Porcupine 37
Porter, General 280, 281
Price, Chas. S............................
............................125*, 19, 194, 196, 238, 303
Put-In-Bay ....
............................135*, 72, 242 to 246, 276

Quedoc 177
Queen Charlotte 38
Queen City 96*, 12
Queen Mary 258
Queen of the West............................12, 62

Ravenscraig 237
Red Crown 229
Regina........124*, 19, 192, 194, 196, 303
Reid, J. T............................129*, 235
Reindeer 96*
Richards, Henry C............85*, 96*, 236

Note: * Indicates illustration.

Rice, R. N. 78
Richelieu 11
Richmond, Dean 61
Rochester 280, 281
Rockefeller, Frank 235
Rogers, Henry H. 222
Roosevelt, Theodore 77, 205, 247
Runnels, H. E. 20, 304
Russell, Roy K. 65
Russia 18, 303

Saginaw 78
Sainte Ignace 249
Sainte Marie 249
Saint Louis 78
Samson 96*, 235
Sand Merchant ....22, 165 to 167, 305
Santa Maria...................161 to 164
Savannah, see City of Savannah
Saxona 193
Scorpion 37, 51
Scott, Isaac M. ....
...................126*, 19, 194, 197, 303
Seabird 14, 302
Seeandbee........133*, 136*, 137*, 19,
..................251, 256 to 266, 268, 271
Shenango 18
Silver Spray .... - 19, 303
Simmons, Rouse 170, 171, 303
Sirius 10, 43
Slocum, General 18
Smith, Henry B. 19, 194, 197, 303
Somers 37
South American 138*, 250
Southerner 78
Southern Michigan 61
South Park 235
State of New York............................ 79
State of Ohio....................21, 75, 79
Ste. Claire 246
Stephenson, I. Watson.....................
....................118*, 232, 233, 234
Stewart, A. E. 192
St. Lawrence 12, 62
Stockbridge, F. B. 90*
Straits of Mackinac 249
Sullivan, J. J. 237
Superior 8, 10, 48
Superior City ....
.........105*, 17, 20, 223, 226, 227, 304
Sweepstakes 235

Tashmoo 117*, 18,
.............22, 72 to 74, 116, 180 to 188
Tempest No. 2....................18, 303
Thistle 193
Thunder Bay Quarries...................165
Tigress 37
Tionesta...............119*, 22, 65 to 67, 80
Titanic 19
Townsend, Charles 48
Townsend, E. Y. 18
Trippe 37
Turret Chief 192

United States 9

Vandalia............96*, 10, 64, 223 to 225
Victory 193
Virginia 78

Waldo, L. C. ....
...............126*, 19, 192, 194, 197, 198
Walk-in-the-Water ....
...................91*, 8, 42 to 48, 223, 224
Walters, Thomas 304
Ward, E. 93*
Ward, Samuel 78
Warner, J. F. 13
Washburn 129*, 235
Washington 10, 302
Watson, Ralph H. 22, 228
Wauketa 72
Wehrle, Jr. A. 113*, 114*, 115*
Westerian 65
Western Metropolis 13, 62
Western States...................79, 216, 252
Western World ....12, 14, 61 to 63
Wexford 127*, 19,
...................192, 194, 196, 198, 303
Whelan, George J. 22, 305
Wilmette, U. S. S. 109*, 201, 202
Wilson, Thomas 18
Windsor 142*
Wisconsin 21, 305
Wolf, Wm. H. 129*
Wolverine 94*, 95*, 11,
...................20, 39, 40, 49 to 57, 64
Wolvin, Augustus B. 224, 227
Woodruff, Lewis 195

Yakima 105*, 237

Note: * Indicates illustration.

NOTES

NOTES

NOTES